Russian for Librarians

Russian for Librarians

AND RUSSIAN BOOKS IN LIBRARIES

Second revised edition

Gregory Walker MA PhD FLA

*Head of Slavonic Section,
Bodleian Library, Oxford*

CLIVE BINGLEY LONDON

Copyright © G P M Walker 1983
First published 1973
· Published by Clive Bingley Limited, 16 Pembridge Road, London W11 3HL, and
printed and bound in England by Redwood Burn Limited, Trowbridge, Wilts.

First published 1973
This second, revised edition published 1983

British Library Cataloguing in Publication Data

Walker, Gregory
    Russian for librarians. — second ed.
    1. Russian language — Grammar — 1950.
    2. Library science
    I. Title
    491.78'002421   PG2112

    ISBN 0-85157-359-2

Typeset by Allset Composition in 10 on 12 point Press Roman

1234586858483

CONTENTS

To Anne, Ruth and Mark

INTRODUCTION TO THE SECOND EDITION

Like the first edition of 1973, this book is intended to assist the handling of Russian publications by librarians in two ways. Firstly, it supplies a short 'traditional' basic grammar of Russian, together with exercises and a Russian-English vocabulary of about 700 words, to help the non-Russian-speaking librarian deal with Russian material in acquisition and cataloguing routines, in serial recording and in the consultation of Russian bibliographical data. These sections are not designed for those needing sufficient Russian for informed book selection, nor for information work based on the content of Russian publications. Still less are they intended to impart the active ability to speak or write correct Russian. Secondly, the book offers sections dealing with specific problems presented to the librarian by Russian books: transliteration, Soviet publishing practice, acquisition, cataloguing, bibliographies and reference works, and the identification of other languages using Cyrillic. Lists of Russian bibliographical and library abbreviations, and of Soviet publishing houses, are appended.

For the second edition, stress marking has been added to Russian words throughout the text, the exercises expanded and some grammatical points amplified. The vocabulary has been recast to give greater emphasis to library and bibliographical terminology. All the non-linguistic sections have been rewritten completely or in part, and that on Soviet publishing practice is entirely new.

As an alternative approach to providing librarians with a basic knowledge of Russian, readers are recommended to compare the chapter on Russian (pp 391-426) in C G Allen's extremely useful work, *A manual of European languages for librarians* (London/New York, Bowker, 1975).

Librarians who wish to make contact with colleagues elsewhere engaged in work with Russian materials can do so through:

In the UK: Advisory Committee on Slavonic and East European Materials of the Standing Conference of National and University Libraries. SCONUL Secretariat: 102 Euston Road, London NW1 2HA.

In North America: Bibliography and Documentation Committee of the American Association for the Advancement of Slavic Studies. Chair (1982): Professor Marianna Tax Choldin, University of Illinois Library, 1408 West Gregory Drive, Urbana, Illinois 61801, USA.

I acknowledge with gratitude the advice and help of the following colleagues in the preparation of the new edition: Jenny Brine (Centre for Russian and East European Studies, University of Birmingham), Nicholas Brown (School of Slavonic and East European Studies, University of London), Chris Thomas and Michael Maclaren-Turner of the British Library Reference Division, Michael Heaney of the Bodleian Library, and Marianna Tax Choldin of the University of Illinois. Responsibility for errors and omissions is of course entirely mine, and corrections will be gratefully received.

Gregory Walker
Slavonic Section
Bodleian Library
December 1982   Oxford OX1 3BG

ABBREVIATIONS

acc.	accusative case
adj.	adjective
adv.	adverb
dat.	dative case
esp.	especially
fem.	feminine gender
gen.	genitive case
instr.	instrumental case
ipfve.	imperfective aspect
loc.	locative case
masc.	masculine gender
neut.	neuter gender
nom.	nominative case
pfve.	perfective aspect
pl.	plural
prep.	preposition
sing., sg.	singular
usu.	usually

Section 1

RUSSIAN COURSE

1.1. Learning Russian

Although Russian is, in terms of its history and structure as a language, related relatively closely to English and to other West European languages, it has unfamiliar features which make it more difficult to learn than, say, German or Spanish for most native English speakers. Although this book is intended only for a limited and specialized study of the language, it will nevertheless introduce the learner to, and give practice in, a number of these unfamiliar characteristics.

The Cyrillic alphabet, in which Russian is written, will probably not prove to be the great obstacle it seems at first sight. A number of the letters are similar to their equivalents in the Roman alphabet (although a few misleading resemblances must be watched for), and others closely resemble letters of the Greek alphabet. An advantage over English is that written Russian gives a much better — though not perfect — indication of its pronunciation: the sound or sounds associated with each letter of the alphabet are regular enough in occurrence to make a comprehensible pronunciation possible by following a minimum of rules. Throughout this course, the exercises should be treated as practice in spelling out, reading and writing Russian, and at a later stage transliterating it into Roman characters.

The structure of Russian makes much greater use than English of variations in word-ending to show differences in the grammatical usage of a word. The notion of gender ('masculine'/'feminine'/'neuter') plays as important a part in Russian as it does in German or Latin, and is likewise reflected in word-endings. These sets of endings ('declensions') are treated here in some detail for Russian nouns, adjectives and pronouns, since their accurate recognition is often important in, for example, the correct citation of an author's name or the understanding of a title-page.

The complications of Russian verb usage, which would need to be tackled at length in acquiring a good general knowledge of Russian, have in this course only been outlined: verbal constructions are much less significant than normal in the variety of Russian met with in simple document handling.

The vocabulary of Russian has fewer obvious points of contact with English than the vocabularies of West European languages, calling perhaps for a rather greater effort of memory. However, this course sets out to give a 'passive' knowledge — that is, the ability to translate in the Russian-to-English direction only — using a strictly limited set of words and phrases, with exercises and examples to show their use in context.

Russian, like all languages, has many irregularities and exceptions to its grammatical rules. The course which follows has been designed to set out the basic rules, noting only some of the most important exceptions and irregularities. A fuller grammar should be consulted for more detailed information.

In working through the course, the vocabularies and exercises given at intervals should be taken unhurriedly and at length by those needing anything more than a nodding acquaintance with the appearance and character of Russian. *Wherever possible, further original material in Russian should be used for close examination and extra practice. Skill will come only with practical experience.*

1.2. Alphabet, script, pronunciation

1.2.1. Alphabet

The Cyrillic alphabet as used in Russian now consists of 33 letters in the order shown below:

Printed cap/lc	Script cap/lc	Name of letter (approximation Anglicized)	Approximate pronunciation	Examples	
А а	*Аа*	ah	*a*rc	а́втор	author
Б б	*Бб*	beh	*b*ed	без	without
В в	*Вв*	veh	*v*an	век	century
Г г	*Гг*	geh	*g*as	год	year
Д д	*Дд*	deh	*d*ot	до	until
Е е	*Ее*	yeh	*y*et	все	all
Ё ё (usually written E, e)	*Ёё*	yo	*y*ore	её	her, hers

13

Printed cap/lc	Script cap/lc	Name of letter (approximation Anglicised)	Approximate pronunciation	Examples	
Ж ж	*Ж ж*	zheh	vi*s*ion	журна́л	journal
З з	*З з*	zeh	*z*one	загла́вие	title
И и	*И и*	ee	v*i*sa	и	and
				из	from
Й й	*Й й*	ee krátkoye ('short ee')	co*i*n	май	May
К к	*К к*	kah	*k*id	как	how
				кни́га	book
Л л	*Л л*	el	woo*l*	глава́	chapter, head
М м	*М м*	em	*m*ap	Москва́	Moscow
Н н	*Н н*	en	*n*ow	не	not
О о	*О о*	oh	*o*re	от	from
П п	*П п*	peh	*p*ot	под	under
Р р	*Р р*	ehr	ki*r*k (Scots)	рома́н	novel
				реда́ктор	editor
С с	*С с*	ess	*s*ea	собра́ние	collection
Т т	*Т т, т*	teh	*t*on	том	volume
У у	*У у*	ooh	r*u*le	университе́т	university
Ф ф	*Ф ф*	eff	*f*at	филиа́л	branch
Х х	*Х х*	kha	lo*ch*	худо́жник	artist
Ц ц	*Ц ц*	tseh	cur*ts*ey	цена́	price
Ч ч	*Ч ч*	cheh	*ch*eek	член	member
Ш ш	*Ш ш, ш*	shah	*sh*ot	шко́ла	school
Щ щ	*Щ щ*	shchah	pu*sh-ch*air	ещё	still, yet
	ъ	*ъ*	tvyórdy znak (= 'hard sign': see 1.2.2.)		
	ы	*ы*	yerý	wh*i*sky (Scots)	мы	we
	ь	*ь*	myákhki znak (= 'soft sign': see 1.2.2.)		
Э э	*Э э*	eh	*e*nd	э́ра	era
Ю ю	*Ю ю*	yu	*yu*le	юг	south
Я я	*Я я*	yah	*ya*rn	язы́к	language

The use of the following letters was discontinued in the Soviet
Union in 1918, but they continued to appear in *émigré* publications
for many years:

	i		*i*	ee	v*i*sa	(now replaced by и)
Ѣ	ѣ	*Ѣ*	*ѣ*	yat'	*ye*t	(now replaced by е)
Ѳ	ѳ	*Ѳ*	*ѳ*	feeta	*f*at	(now replaced by ф)
V	v	*V*	*v*	izhitsa	v*i*sa	(now replaced by и)

Note that the appearance of these letters in Cyrillic alphabetical listings
(eg indexes, bibliographies, encyclopaedias) will mean that a word containing any of them will appear in an alphabetical location *different*
from that which it would occupy when spelt in the modern (Soviet)
alphabet. This most commonly affects words formerly spelt with ѣ,
which filed before э, and are now spelt with e.

1.2.2. 'Hard' and 'soft' signs

ъ and ь indicate variations in the pronunciation of the preceding sound
or sounds. ь indicates a 'palatalization', which can often be roughly
reproduced by inserting a slight -y- sound, eg:

ть	has about the quality of *t* in *t*ube:	шесть	six
нь	has about the quality of *n* in *n*ew:	пéречень	list
сь	has about the quality of *s* in He*ss*ian:	письмó	letter

ъ is now only occasionally used, to show the absence of a 'palatalization' where it might otherwise be expected. Until 1917, however, it was
regularly used, though not pronounced, at the end of all words not
ending in a vowel or the 'soft sign', eg отъ (now от), годъ (now год).
Note that, as in the case of other obsolete letters, the occurrence of ъ
will result in a different alphabetical filing order from the modern one.

1.2.3. Learning the alphabet
Notice that:
1. These letters are *usefully* similar to English letters in pronunciation:

A	Б (= b)	Д (= d)	E	З (= z)	К	М	O
		С (= s)	T	Э (= e)			

2. These are *misleadingly* similar to English:

В (= v *not* B)   И (= i *not* N)   H (= N *not* H)
P (= R *not* P)   У (= U *not* y)   X (= kh *not* x)
ъ and ь ('hard' and 'soft' signs, *not* b)

ы (short i, one sound only, nothing to so with ь or b)

Я (= ya *not* R)

3. These letters are usefully similar to Greek:

Γ (= g)   Д (= d)   Л (= L)   П (= p)   Р (= r)   Ф (= f)

4. Learn to distinguish between these groups:

б (= b), в (= v), р (= r), ъ ('hard sign'), ь ('soft sign'), ы (short i),
ѣ (pre-1918, = e);

ж (= zh), х (= kh);

л (= l), п (= p), ц (= ts), ч (= ch), ш (= sh), щ (= shch);

у (= u), ч (= ch).

1.2.4. Script

The examples below show the method of joining letters in cursive script. Note that the italic type faces (examples shown later in the book) resemble written Cyrillic closely.

почта, / *почта*	по́чта	post (ie mail)
имени	и́мени	named after
большевик	большеви́к	Bolshevik
Ленинград	Ленингра́д	Leningrad
библиография	библиогра́фия	bibliography
должно быть / *должно быть*	должно́ быть	should be
сельскохозяйственный	сельскохозяйст-венный	agricultural
отъ редакціи	отъ реда́кціи	from the editors (pre- 1918)
от редакции	от реда́кции	from the editors (post- 1918)
въ Европѣ	въ Евро́пѣ	in Europe (pre- 1918)
в Европе	в Евро́пе	in Europe (post- 1918)

Print out and write in script all the Russian words introduced so far and arrange them in *Russian* alphabetical order, covering up the key below (as in subsequent exercises) until you give up.

áвтор	author	от	from, away from
без	without		
библиогрáфия	bibliography	пéречень	list
большевúк	Bolshevik	письмó	letter
в	in, into	под	under
век	century, age	пóлный	full
все	all	пóчта	post
главá	chapter	редáктор	editor
год	year	редáкция	editorship, editorial staff
до	until, up to		
должнó быть	should be	ромáн	novel
Еврóпа	Europe	сельскохозя́йст-	agricultural
еë	her(s)	венный	
ещë	still, yet	собрáние	collection
журнáл	journal	том	volume
заглáвие	title	университéт	university
и	and	филиáл	branch
из	from, out of	худóжник	artist
úмени	named after	ценá	price
как	how	член	member
кнúга	book	шесть	six
Ленингрáд	Leningrad	шкóла	school
май	May	э́ра	era
Москвá	Moscow	юг	south
мы	we	язы́к	language
не	not		

1.2.5. Stress

The stressed syllable in Russian varies from word to word as in English, and also from one form of the same word to another, eg in the different persons of a verb conjugation. The pronunciation of unstressed vowels is often much slackened or slurred. Unstressed o, for example, is frequently sounded very like a. Throughout this book, stressed syllables are marked with an acute accent (eg áвтор), but this stress marking is *never* used in normal printed or written Russian.

1.3. Articles, gender and case

1.3.1. Articles

There are no definite or indefinite articles in Russian. кни́га may need to be translated as '*the* book', '*a* book', or simply 'book', according to the context.

1.3.2. Gender

Russian nouns are classified into masculine, feminine and neuter *genders*, with gender usually determined by the ending of the word.

Masculine
nouns ending in a consonant: лист 'leaf, sheet', коне́ц 'end';
nouns ending in -й: музе́й 'museum', Кита́й 'China';
some nouns ending in -ь: слова́рь 'dictionary', чита́тель 'reader'.

Feminine
nouns ending in -a: газе́та 'newspaper', нау́ка 'science, scholarship';
nouns ending in -я: поэ́зия 'poetry', па́ртия 'party';
most nouns ending in -ь: печа́ть 'press'.

Neuter
nouns ending in -o: сло́во 'word', изда́тельство 'publishing house';
nouns ending in -e: введе́ние 'introduction', сочине́ние 'work,
  composition';
a few nouns ending in -мя: вре́мя 'time'.

EXERCISE 2

As with Exercise 1, print out, write in script and arrange in Russian alphabetical order words introduced since that point.

введе́ние	introduction	печа́ть	press
изда́тельство	publishing-house	поэ́зия	poetry
Кита́й	China	слова́рь	dictionary
коне́ц	end	сло́во	word
лист	leaf, sheet	сочине́ние	work, compo-
нау́ка	science,		sition
	scholarship	чита́тель	reader
па́ртия	party*		

*in Soviet contexts, usually the Communist Party of the Soviet Union

18

1.3.3. Case

Russian nouns, adjectives and pronouns occur in six *case* forms according to their grammatical function, as in Latin and, to a lesser extent, German. The use of each is illustrated below.

Nominative: the case of the subject of a sentence, regarded as the 'standard' form and hence that shown in, for example, dictionary entries.

'*Кни́жная ле́топись*' издаётся с 1907 го́да.
'*Book chronicle*' has been published since the year 1907.

Сле́дующие кни́ги вы́шли из печа́ти.
The following books have gone out from the press [ie been published].

Accusative: the case of the direct object of a sentence. Also used after some prepositions.

Перево́д с англи́йского подгото́вил Л. С. Па́влов.
[The] *translation* from English prepared L. S. Pavlov
(Note the inversion of the usual English word order here, made possible — apart from the sense, as here — by the use of word *form* instead of word *order* to show grammatical function.)

Genitive: The case showing possession ('whose?' or 'of what?'). Also used after many prepositions. In both functions very frequently met in document handling.

День *поэ́зии*.
[the] Day *of Poetry* (genitive singular of поэ́зия).

собра́ние *сочине́ний*.
collection *of works* (genitive plural of сочине́ние).

план *вы́пуска литерату́ры*.
plan *of issue of literature* (ie 'forthcoming titles'. Genitive singular of вы́пуск and литерату́ра).

резюме́ *стате́й*.
summary *of articles* (genitive plural of статья́).

от нача́ла до конца́
from beginning to end (both prepositions take the genitive. Genitive singular of нача́ло and коне́ц respectively).

Dative: the case of the indirect object ('to whom?' or 'to what?'). Also used after a few prepositions.

вся власть *Совётам!*
all power *to the Soviets!* (dative plural of **Совёт**).

приложе́ние *к журна́лу*
supplement *to [the] journal.* (к takes dative. Dative singular of
  журна́л).

Instrumental: the case of the instrument or agent ('by whom?', 'by what?'). Also used after some prepositions.

сбо́рник соста́влен *коллекти́вом*
[the] symposium [is/was] compiled *by a collective.* (Instrumental
  singular of коллекти́в. Note that the present tense of the
  Russian verb 'to be' is usually omitted. Despite the consequent
  telegraphic appearance, the sense of what remains is normally
  clear.)

Locative (or Prepositional): used only after a small number of prepositions, some of which indicate position and all of which are common,
eg о 'about'; на 'on, in'; в 'in'; при 'at'.

на ру́сском языке́,
in [the] Russian language (locative singular of ру́сский язы́к).

в трёх тома́х.
in three volumes (locative plural of три and том).

EXERCISE 3

Write out and arrange new words as before. The key is given below.

англи́йский	English	к	(with dat.)
власть	power		to, up to
вся	all (variant of	кни́жный	book (adj.)
	все, see 1.8.3)	коллекти́в	collective
вы́пуск	issue	ле́топись	chronicle,
вы́шли	went/have		annals
	gone out	литерату́ра	literature (not
день	day		necessarily
и́збранный	selected		fiction)
издаётся	is being/has been	на	(with loc.)
	published		on, in

нача́ло	beginning	с	(with gen.)
о	(with loc.)		from, off
	about	сбо́рник	symposium,
перево́д	translation		collection of
план	plan		articles
подгото́вил	prepared	сле́дующий	following
при	(with loc.) at	сове́т	soviet, council
приложе́ние	supplement	соста́вленный	compiled
резюме́	summary	статья́	article
ру́сский	Russian	три	three

1.4. Noun declension

Do not be put off by the apparently formidable table of variant endings on page 22. Study it carefully, using the notes as a guide to recognizing the regularities as well as the aberrations.

The most important regularity is that all three genders have parallel 'hard' and 'soft' declensions which are basically alike but differ in the vowel sound of their endings. Thus, in the fem., пье́са, declined 'hard', has acc. and gen. пье́су and пье́сы, whereas неде́ля, declined 'soft', shows the endings неде́лю and неде́ли. This correspondence of sounds can be followed throughout the declensions as an aid to learning.

Other notable similarities are those between the masculine and neuter declensions almost throughout, and in the dat., instr. and loc. plural, where the 'hard' and 'soft' ending sets -ам, -ами, -ах and -ям, -ями, -ях appear in all three genders.

With these likenesses in mind, attention can be paid to deviations such as the extra declension for feminine nouns ending in the soft sign -ь, the 'animate'/'inanimate' distinction in the acc. sing. masculine and the accusative plural, and the complete disappearance of endings in the feminine and neuter genitive plural.

		MASCULINE		FEMININE			NEUTER	
		'language'	'museum'	'play'	'week'	'speech'	'place'	'edition'
Singular	Nom.	язы́к	музе́й	пье́са	неде́ля	речь	ме́сто	изда́ние
	Acc.	if animate noun, like gen.; else like nom.		пье́су	неде́лю	речь	ме́сто	изда́ние
	Gen.	языка́	музе́я	пье́сы	неде́ли	ре́чи	ме́ста	изда́ния
	Dat.	языку́	музе́ю	пье́се	неде́ле	ре́чи	ме́сту	изда́нию
	Instr.	языко́м	музе́ем	пье́сой	неде́лей	ре́чью	ме́стом	изда́нием
	Loc.	языке́	музе́е	пье́се	неде́ле	ре́чи	ме́сте	изда́нии
Plural	Nom.	языки́	музе́и	пье́сы	неде́ли	ре́чи	места́	изда́ния
	Acc.	[if animate noun, like genitive. If inanimate, like nominative]					места́	изда́ния
	Gen.	языко́в	музе́ев	пьес	неде́ль	рече́й	мест	изда́ний
	Dat.	языка́м	музе́ям	пье́сам	неде́лям	реча́м	места́м	изда́ниям
	Instr.	языка́ми	музе́ями	пье́сами	неде́лями	реча́ми	места́ми	изда́ниями
	Loc.	языка́х	музе́ях	пье́сах	неде́лях	реча́х	места́х	изда́ниях

Notes:

1. In the accusative case, the masculine singular and all genders in the plural use the genitive form for nouns denoting living creatures. Otherwise the nominative form is used.

2. Neuter nouns ending in -ие and feminine nouns ending in -ия have the endings -и in the locative singular and -ий in the genitive plural; eg реце́нзия 'review' has the gen. pl. реце́нзий as in Ле́топись реце́нзий 'Chronicle of reviews', and загла́вие 'title, heading' has gen. pl. загла́вий as in указа́тель загла́вий 'index of titles'.

3. Many masculine nouns lose the last vowel of the stem in oblique (ie other than nominative) cases, eg день, gen. sing. дня, nom. pl. дни; коне́ц, gen. sing. конца́; спи́сок 'list', gen. sing. спи́ска; рису́нок 'drawing, figure' as in с рису́нками 'with drawings' (с with instrumental = 'with'); иностра́нец 'foreigner' as in для иностра́нцев 'for foreigners' (для with genitive = 'for').

4. Where masculine nouns end in г, ж, к, х, ч, ш ог щ, the nominative plural ending is -и not -ы, even though the declension is otherwise 'hard', eg ве́стник 'bulletin', nom. pl. ве́стники; ито́г 'result', nom. pl. ито́ги; о́черк 'outline, sketch', nom. pl. о́черки; стих 'verse', nom. pl. стихи́ 'poetry'; тира́ж 'size of edition', nom. pl. тиражи́.

5. Likewise, where feminine nouns end in га, жа, ка, ха, ча, ша ог ща, the genitive singular and nominative plural endings are -и, not -ы, although the declension is otherwise 'hard', eg кни́га 'book', gen. sing. and nom. pl. кни́ги; библиоте́ка/библиоте́ки 'library'; запи́ска/запи́ски 'note' (in pl. 'notes' or 'transactions').

EXERCISE 4

List new words as before. The key is given below.

акаде́мия	academy	ме́сто	place
библиоте́ка	library	о́черк	outline, sketch
ве́стник	bulletin; messenger	пье́са	play
		реце́нзия	review
для	(with gen.) for	речь	speech
запи́ска	note;(in pl.: notes, transactions)	рису́нок	drawing, figure
		спи́сок	list
изда́ние	edition; impression; publication	стих	verse; (pl. poetry)
		тира́ж	size of edition, no. of copies
иностра́нец	foreigner		
ито́г	result	указа́тель	index

Translate the following into English. (All words have been introduced previously in the course and case endings can be identified from the table on page 22.)

1. Ру́сский язы́к в шко́ле.
2. Цена́ кни́ги.
3. А́втор реце́нзии.
4. Библиоте́ка и́мени В. И. Ле́нина.
5. Введе́ние к рома́ну.
6. Без цены́ (б. ц.)
7. От Москвы́ до Ленингра́да.
8. Письма́ А. С. Пу́шкина.
9. Под реда́кции коллекти́ва.
10. Рома́н в стиха́х.
11. От изда́тельства.
12. Поэ́зия Кита́я.
13. Па́ртия о печа́ти.
14. Статьи́ о худо́жниках.
15. Ве́стник Акаде́мии Нау́к.
16. Указа́тель загла́вий.
17. Без ме́ста изда́ния. (б. м.).
18. Изда́ние с рису́нками И. Я. Били́бина.
19. Спи́сок книг.

Key:
1. [The] Russian language in [the] school. (в: prep. with locative).
2. The price of the book. (кни́га in genitive).
3. The author of the review. (реце́нзия in genitive).
4. Library named after V. I. Lenin. (и́мени followed by gen.).
5. Introduction to the novel. (к followed by dat. singular of рома́н).
6. Without price (unpriced). (без: prep. with genitive).
7. From Moscow to Leningrad. (Both preps. take genitive).
8. [The] letters of A. S. Pushkin.
9. Under the editorship of a collective. (под with instrumental).
10. [A] novel in verse. (в followed by locative pl. of стих).
11. From the publisher. (от: prep. with genitive).
12. [The] poetry of China. (Genitive of Кита́й).
13. [The] Party on the press. (о followed by loc. sing. of печа́ть).
14. Articles on artists. (о followed by loc. pl.)

15. Bulletin of the Academy of Sciences. (Акадéмия in gen. sing., Наýка in gen. pl.).
16. Index of titles. (Gen. pl. of заглáвие).
17. Without [a] place of publication.
18. Edition [*or* publication] with drawings of I. Ya. Bilibin. (c followed by instr. plural of рисýнок).
19. List of books. (Gen. pl. of кнйга).

1.5. Adjectives and adverbs

1.5.1. Attributive adjectives

Adjectives agree with the noun they qualify in number, gender and case, as in French, German and Latin. When used attributively (eg 'the *red* book'), they usually precede the noun, as in English. When used predicatively (eg 'the book is *red*'), they often appear in a shortened form (see 1.5.2).

Adjectives in the singular have one basic form for *each* gender. In the plural, there is one basic declension applying to *all* genders. The precise form of the ending varies according to the 'hard' or 'soft' pronunciation of the consonant before it, in a similar way to the noun declensions.

	Singular MASCULINE	FEMININE	NEUTER	*Plural* ALL GENDERS
Nom.	нóв*ый* 'new'	нóв*ая*	нóв*ое*	нóв*ые*
Acc.	[like nom. or gen., as nouns]	нóв*ую*	нóв*ое*	[like nom. or gen., as nouns]
Gen.	нóв*ого*	нóв*ой*	нóв*ого*	нóв*ых*
Dat.	нóв*ому*	нóв*ой*	нóв*ому*	нóв*ым*
Instr.	нóв*ым*	нóв*ой*, нóв*ою*	нóв*ым*	нóв*ыми*
Loc.	нóв*ом*	нóв*ой*	нóв*ом*	нóв*ых*

Notes:

1. Masculine and neuter adjectives are declined identically in the singular, except in the nom./acc.
2. Adjectives which are stressed on the ending have the form -óй in the nominative masc. singular, but are otherwise declined as above. Examples: большóй 'great', другóй 'other(s)'.

3. The ending -ого (or -его) in the masc. and neuter genitive singular is pronounced *in these endings only* as -ово (or -ево).
4. Before 1918, the endings -аго/-яго were normally used instead of -ого/-его in the masc. and neut. gen. sing., and the endings -ыя/-ія instead of the modern -ые/-ие in the nom./acc. plural.

EXERCISE 5

New adjectives. (These have *not* all been mentioned before. Most are supplied in this list for the first time.)

алфави́тный	alphabetical	иностра́нный	foreign (cf. иностра́нец foreigner)
библиографи́ческий	bibliographical		
большо́й	great	истори́ческий	historical (cf. исто́рия history)
ва́жный	important		
вели́кий	great		
восто́чный	eastern (cf. восто́к east)	коммунисти́ческий	Communist (adj.)
вы́сший	higher	кра́ткий	short
гла́вный	main, chief (cf. глава́ chapter; head)	моско́вский	Muscovite (cf. Москва́ Moscow)
		музыка́льный	musical (cf. му́зыка music)
госуда́рственный	state (adj.)		
де́тский	children's (cf. де́ти children)	нау́чный	scientific, scholarly
друго́й	other(s)	не́который	some, certain
за́падный	western (cf. за́пад west)	но́вый	new

Translate into English.

1. Кра́ткий о́черк ру́сской исто́рии.
2. Не́которые ва́жные изда́ния.
3. 'Истори́ческие запи́ски'.
4. Алфави́тный спи́сок библиогра́фий для вы́сших школ.
5. Де́тская литерату́ра.
6. Гла́вный реда́ктор сбо́рника.

7. Изда́ние подгото́вил Л. В. Миха́йлов и други́е.
8. Указа́тель иностра́нных слов.

Key:
1. Short outline of Russian history. (Gen. sing. forms of ру́сская исто́рия).
2. Some important editions [*or* publications]. (Nom. plural throughout).
3. 'Historical notes'. (Title of an important irregular series).
4. Alphabetical list of bibliographies for higher schools [ie universities]. (Gen. pl. of библиогра́фия, and gen. pl. of вы́сшая шко́ла after preposition для).
5. Children's literature.
6. Chief editor of the symposium.
7. L. V. Mikhailov and others prepared the publication [*or* edition]. (Inversion of subject and object).
8. Index of foreign words.

1.5.2. Predicative adjectives

Many Russian adjectives have a shortened form which is used (in the nominative only) where the verb 'to be' occurs or is implied in the type of construction 'the book *is red*'. Since in Russian the verb 'to be' is usually omitted in the present tense — or shown by a dash — the result is often a noun followed by the shortened form of the adjective. See the example for 'compiled' below.

	Long form	*Short form*
nom. masc. sing.	соста́вленный	соста́влен
nom. fem. sing.	соста́вленная	соста́влена
nom. neuter sing.	соста́вленное	соста́влено
nom. plural	соста́вленные	соста́влены

Compare:
a. 1967 соста́вленный вы́пуск 'the issue compiled [in] 1967'.
b. э́тот сбо́рник соста́влен А. Н. Ша́нским 'this symposium is [*or* has been] compiled by A. N. Shanskii'. (Note adjectival ending of Ша́нский, here in instr.).

Note that соста́вленный is, strictly, a past participle passive (see 1.10.6), not an adjective. The short form of adjectival ending is often encountered where these participles occur in bibliographical data or title-page wording.

New adjectives. (See note to Exercise 5.)

неме́цкий	German	рабо́чий	working, worker (declined as adj., ie 'working person')
о́бщий	general, common		
отде́льный	separate (cf. отде́л section, department)		
после́дний	last, latest	се́верный	northern (cf. се́вер north)
предме́тный	subject (adj., cf. предме́т subject)	францу́зский	French
		центра́льный	central
		ю́жный	southern (cf. юг south)

New nouns.

бюллете́нь	bulletin	произведе́ние	work, production
вопро́с	question, matter	содержа́ние	contents
го́род (pl. города́)	town	спра́вочник	handbook, guide
изве́стия	(neut. pl.) news, 'transactions'	СССР (= Сою́з Сове́тских Социалисти́ческих Респу́блик)	USSR (= Union of Soviet Socialist Republics)
комите́т	committee		
наро́д	people, nation		
писа́тель	writer	студе́нт	student
пра́вда	truth	те́хника	technology

Translate into English.

1. Ру́сско-неме́цкий математи́ческий слова́рь.
2. О́бщие вопро́сы те́хники.
3. Центра́льный комите́т Коммунисти́ческой па́ртии Сове́тского Сою́за (ЦК КПСС).
4. Францу́зский рабо́чий класс и сове́тский наро́д.
5. Бюллете́нь Институ́та ру́сского языка́ при Моско́вском госуда́рственном университе́те (МГУ).

6. Предме́тный указа́тель к библиогра́фии.
7. Сою́з писа́телей СССР.
8. Спра́вочник издаётся Акаде́мией нау́к под реда́кцией комите́та специали́стов.

Key:
1. Russian-German mathematical dictionary.
2. General questions of technology.
3. Central Committee of the Communist Party of the Soviet Union.
4. The French working class and the Soviet people.
5. Bulletin of the Institute of Russian Language at Moscow State University. (при taking locative case).
6. Subject index to the bibliography. (к with dative).
7. Union of Writers of the USSR.
8. The handbook is being published by the Academy of Sciences under the editorship of a committee of specialists.

1.5.3. Comparison of adjectives

The *comparative* form of an adjective (eg high*er*) is expressed in two ways:
a. Used attributively, by adding бо́лее 'more' or ме́нее 'less' before the basic adjective, eg бо́лее ва́жное де́ло 'a more important matter'. A few attributive comparatives end in -ший and are declined like other adjectives. Some of these also have a superlative meaning. They include:

вы́сший	higher, highest	(высо́кий	high)
лу́чший	better, best	(хоро́ший	good)
ме́ньший	smaller	(ма́ленький	small)
ста́рший	older, eldest	(ста́рый	old)

b. Used predicatively, by giving the adjective the invariable ending -ee, eg мо́е де́ло ва́жнее ва́шего, or мо́е де́ло ва́жнее, чем ва́ше 'my business is more important than yours'.

The *superlative* of an adjective (high*est*) can be formed in two ways:
   i. Using са́мый before the adjective, agreeing with it in number, gender and case, eg са́мая ре́дкая кни́га 'the rarest book'.
   ii. Altering the ending of the adjective to -айший or -ейший, which is then declined in the usual way, eg нове́йшая кни́га

'the newest book'. (This ending may not have a superlative meaning in the strict sense: the same phrase might carry the sense of 'a (*or* the) very new book'.)

1.5.4. Adverbs

Many adverbs are derived from adjectives by a simple alteration in the ending (cf. English bad/bad*ly*). This is usually to -o (eg ежегóдный 'annual' (adj.), ежегóдно 'annually'), but for 'soft' adjectives to -e.

Adjectives ending in -ский yield adverbs ending in -ски, eg истори́ческий 'historical', истори́чески 'historically'. A special usage is the prefixing of по- to an adverb in -ски to mean 'in the manner, or language, of . . .', eg по-англи́йски 'in English', по-ру́сски 'in Russian'.

EXERCISE 7
New words.

бóлее	more	осóбенно	especially
ваш	your(s)	повтóрно	again
включи́тельно	inclusive(ly)	рéдкий	rare
высóкий	high	сáмый	most;
вы́сший	higher, highest		the very . . .;
дéло	affair, matter,		same
	business	совремéнный	contemporary
ежегóдно	annually	стáрый	old
ежемéсячно	monthly (adv.)	стáрший	older, oldest
еженедéльно	weekly (adv.)	страни́ца	page
лу́чший	better, best	так	so, thus
мáленький	small	тáкже	also, as well
мéнее	less	тóже	also, as well
мéньший	smaller	тóлько	only
мнóго	(indeclinable,	ужé	already
	with gen.)	хорóший	good
	much, many	чем	than
нéсколько	(indeclinable,		
	with gen.)		
	several, a few,		
	some		

Translate into English.

1. Не́сколько томо́в но́вого изда́ния А. П. Че́хова — уже́ в Нау́чной библиоте́ке университе́та.
2. Се́веро-восто́чная А́зия в совреме́нной сове́тской литерату́ре: рекоменда́тельная библиогра́фия.
3. Ре́дкие кни́ги неме́цких изда́тельств: анноти́рованный катало́г.
4. Указа́тель загла́вий — на стр.[ана́х] 432-448 вкл.[ючи́тельно].
5. Кни́га сост.[а́влена] А. С. Волко́нским и др. [уги́ми].
6. Но́вые изда́ния осо́бенно ва́жных ста́рых произведе́ний.

Key:

1. Several volumes of the new edition of A. P. Chekhov [are] already in the Scientific [*or* Research] Library of the university. (не́сколько is invariable and followed by gen.).
2. North-Eastern Asia in contemporary Soviet literature: a recommendatory bibliography.
3. Rare books of [*or* from] German publishers: an annotated catalogue.
4. An index of titles [is] on pages 432-448 inclusive.
5. The book [is *or* has been] compiled by A. S. Volkonskii and others.
6. New editions of especially important old works.

1.6. Personal names

Russian personal names have traditionally had three components — forename (и́мя); patronymic (о́тчество, derived from the father's forename); and surname (фами́лия). This three-part name has now become standard in the Soviet Union, even for nationalities among whom it was not previously customary. Examples are:

Ле́в Никола́евич Толсто́й   Влади́мир Ильи́ч Улья́нов (Ле́нин).

А́нна Андре́евна Ахма́това   Ибраги́м Абдулла́евич Азизбе́ков.

Серге́й Ната́нович Бе́рнштейн   О́льга Васи́льевна Лепеши́нская.

With certain exceptions (perhaps the most frequently met being surnames of Ukranian origin ending in -енко, which are indeclinable, such as Шевче́нко, Кириле́нко), all parts of the personal name are declined, either as nouns, as adjectives (in surnames with adjectival endings like

Толсто́й or Ша́нский), or (in surnames with the common endings -ов, -ев and -ин) in a 'mixed' part-noun, part-adjective declension:

	MASCULINE		FEMININE	
Nom.	Козло́в,	Пу́шкин	Козло́ва,	Пу́шкина
Acc.	Козло́ва,	Пу́шкина	Козло́ву,	Пу́шкину
Gen.	Козло́ва,	Пу́шкина	Козло́вой,	Пу́шкиной
Dat.	Козло́ву,	Пу́шкину	Козло́вой,	Пу́шкиной
Instr.	Козло́вым,	Пу́шкиным	Козло́вой,	Пу́шкиной
Loc.	Козло́ве,	Пу́шкине	Козло́вой,	Пу́шкиной

	PLURAL	
Nom.	Козло́вы,	Пу́шкины
Acc.	Козло́вых,	Пу́шкиных
Gen.	Козло́вых,	Пу́шкиных
Dat.	Козло́вым,	Пу́шкиным
Instr.	Козло́выми,	Пу́шкиными
Loc.	Козло́вых,	Пу́шкиных

Adjectival forms of endings are in *italics*. Notice that the accusative form in the plural and masc. singular is always the same as the genitive, since surnames will always, of course, refer to 'animate objects'!

1.7. Numerals

1.7.1. Cardinal and ordinal numerals

	Cardinal numerals ('one', etc.)	Ordinal numerals ('first', etc.)
1	оди́н, одна́, одно́	пе́рвый
2	два, две	второ́й
3	три	тре́тий
4	четы́ре	четвёртый
5	пять	пя́тый

Cardinal numerals ('one', etc.)	Ordinal numerals ('first', etc.)
6 шесть	шестóй
7 семь	седьмóй
8 вóсемь	восьмóй
9 дéвять	девя́тый
10 дéсять	деся́тый
11 оди́ннадцать	одиннáдцатый
12 двенáдцать	двенáдцатый
13 тринáдцать	тринáдцатый
14 четы́рнадцать	четы́рнадцатый
15 пятнáдцать	пятнáдцатый
16 шестнáдцать	шестнáдцатый
17 семнáдцать	семнáдцатый
18 восемнáдцать	восемнáдцатый
19 девятнáдцать	девятнáдцатый
20 двáдцать	двадцáтый
21 двáдцать оди́н	двáдцать пéрвый
22 двáдцать два	двáдцать вторóй
30 три́дцать	тридцáтый
40 сóрок	сороковóй
50 пятьдеся́т	пятидеся́тый
60 шестьдеся́т	шестидеся́тый
70 сéмьдесят	семидеся́тый
80 вóсемьдесят	восьмидеся́тый
90 девянóсто	девянóстый
100 сто	сóтый
200 двéсти	двухсóтый
300 три́ста	трёхсóтый
400 четы́реста	четырёхсóтый
500 пятьсóт	пятисóтый
600 шестьсóт	шестисóтый
700 семьсóт	семисóтый

Cardinal numerals ('one', etc.)		Ordinal numerals ('first', etc.)
800	восемьсо́т	восьмисо́тый
900	девятьсо́т	девятисо́тый
1000	ты́сяча	ты́сячный
2000	две ты́сячи	двухты́сячный
5000	пять ты́сяч	пятиты́сячный

'one-half' = полови́на   'one-third' = треть

'one-quarter' = че́тверть

'the year nineteen sixty-eight' = ты́сяча девятьсо́т шестьдеся́т восьмо́й год, 1968 г.

1.7.2. Declension of numerals

All numerals vary their form according to their grammatical function, like nouns and adjectives. Declension of cardinals in most cases closely resembles one or other of the noun declensions, and oblique forms are usually quite recognizable, with the following possible exceptions:

	2	3	4
Nom.	два, две	три	четы́ре
Acc.		[like nominative or genitive]	
Gen.	двух	трёх	четырёх
Dat.	двум	трём	четырём
Instr.	двумя́	тремя́	четырьмя́
Loc.	двух	трёх	четырёх

1.7.3. Case forms following numerals

Except where they appear in the nominative, numerals agree in case with the nouns and adjectives to which they apply, eg в трёх отде́льных тома́х 'in three separate volumes' (locative case following в).

But:

a. два, три, четы́ре in the *nominative* case are followed by nouns *in the genitive singular* and *adjectives in the genitive plural*, eg три други́х вопро́са 'three other questions' (gen. pl. of друго́й, gen. sing. of вопро́с).

b. Numerals from пять onwards in the *nominative* case are followed by *nouns and adjectives in the genitive plural*, eg шесть дре́вних городо́в 'six ancient towns' (gen. plurals of дре́вний and го́род).

1.7.4. Roman numerals

In Russian usage, Roman numerals are quite commonly met with, especially in the numbering of volumes, centuries and Communist Party conferences, eg том VI 'Volume 6'; XIX-XXвв. '19th-20th centuries'; XXVII съезд КПСС 'the 27th Congress of the CPSU'. Note that, in Cyrillic typescript, it is usual to reproduce Roman numerals by their nearest Cyrillic equivalents, with the result that XVIII, for example, is typed as ХУШ, and may not be immediately recognized.

EXERCISE 8

New words associated with numerals.

до н.э. [на́шей э́ры]	B.C. ('up to our era')	середи́на	middle
копе́йка	kopek (1/100 of a rouble)	се́рия	series
		се́ссия	session
		созы́в	convocation
ле́та	(gen. pl. лет) years. (cf. год which also = year.)*	столе́тие	century (cf. век, also = century)
		съезд	congress
но́мер, №	number; issue	фунт	pound (£)
н.э. [на́шей э́ры]	A.D. ('of our era')	ци́фра	figure
		часть	part
раз	(gen. pl. also раз) time, occasion	экземпля́р	copy, specimen
рубль	rouble		

* The distinction is not explained here, since it chiefly affects translation *into* Russian.

Translate into English.

1. Екатери́на Втора́я.
2. Ф. М. Достое́вский: и́збранные произведе́ния в восьми́ тома́х.
3. Изве́стия Акаде́мии Нау́к СССР [АН СССР]. Се́рия исто́рия, вы́пуск тре́тий [вып. 3-ий].
4. Рабо́чий класс в Донба́ссе в тридца́тых года́х.
5. Рома́н в пе́рвой полови́не девятна́дцатого ве́ка.

6. Цена — три фу́нта, т.е. [то есть, ie] четы́ре рубля́ пятьдеся́т копе́ек.
7. Тира́ж де́сять ты́сяч экземпля́ров [экз.].
8. Верхо́вный (= supreme) Сове́т СССР: тре́тья се́ссия четвёртого созы́ва.
9. Газе́та издаётся шесть раз в неде́ле, а библиогра́фия раз в год.

Key:
1. Catherine the Second (the Great, 1729-96).
2. F. M. Dostoevskii: selected works in eight volumes.
3. News [*or* Transactions] of the Academy of Sciences of the USSR. Series 'History', third issue. (Inversion of phrases with ordinal numbers, like the last two words, is common.)
4. The working class in the Donbas (Donets Basin) in the thirtieth years (ie the Thirties).
5. The novel in the first half of the nineteenth century.
6. The price [is] three pounds, ie four roubles fifty kopeks. (Note that рубль is masc., and рубля́ is thus a 'soft' masc. gen. *sing.* ending after четы́ре. копе́ек is genitive *plural* after '50'.)
7. Size of edition [*or* impression] ten thousand copies.
8. Supreme Soviet of the USSR: third session of the fourth convocation.
9. The newspaper is published six times a week, and the bibliography once a year.

1.8. Pronouns

1.8.1. Personal pronouns ('I', 'you', etc) ───────────

	I	you	he, it	she	we	you (pl.)	they
Nom.	я	ты	он, оно́	она́	мы	вы	они́
Acc.	меня́	тебя́	его́	её	нас	вас	их
Gen.	меня́	тебя́	его́	её	нас	вас	их
Dat.	мне	тебе́	ему́	ей	нам	вам	им
Instr.	мной	тобо́й	им	е́ю	на́ми	ва́ми	и́ми
Loc.	мне	тебе́	нём	ней	нас	вас	них

Notes:
1. Where preceded by a preposition, the oblique variants of он, она́, оно́, они́ are prefixed by н-, eg у него́, для них, с ним, о нём.
2. его́ is pronounced as ево́, as in the adjectival ending.

1.8.2. Possessive pronouns ('my', 'your', etc)

мой,	моя́,	мое́,	мои́	my	⎫
твой,	твоя́,	твое́,	твои́	your	⎪ fully declined, like
свой,	своя́,	свое́,	свои́	one's own	⎬ adjectives
наш,	на́ша,	на́ше,	на́ши	our	⎪
ваш,	ва́ша,	ва́ше,	ва́ши	your	⎭
его́				his, its	⎫ not declined, being
её				her, its	⎬ genitive forms of the personal pronouns
их				their	⎭ in 1.8.1.

1.8.3. Other pronouns

The most important of these are кто 'who', что 'what' and весь 'all'.

Nom.	кто 'who'	что 'what' (pronounced што)
Acc.	кого́	что
Gen.	кого́	чего́
Dat.	кому́	чему́
Instr.	кем	чем
Loc.	ком	чём

весь is declined in all three genders in the singular:

	Masculine	Feminine	Neuter	Plural
Nom.	весь	вся	всё	все
Acc.	весь, всего́	всю	всё	все, всех
Gen.	всего́	всей	всего́	всех
Dat.	всему́	всей	всему́	всем
Instr.	всем	всей	всем	все́ми
Loc.	всём	всей	всём	всех

1.9. Prepositions

Prepositions (eg English 'to', 'by', 'for') in Russian oblige the use of various cases for the nouns, adjectives and pronouns which they govern, eg:

кро́ме э́того	'besides this'	(кро́ме governs the genitive)
к э́тому	'towards this'	(к governs the dative).

Some prepositions govern more than one case, with differing meanings, eg:

в библиоте́ке	*in* the library'	(в governing the locative), *but*
в библиоте́ку	*into* the library'	(в governing the accusative).

Several prepositions alter their form where this is felt necessary for easier pronunciation:

в   may appear as во

к   may appear as ко

с   may appear as со

о   may appear as об, о́бо

The most common Russian prepositions are listed below, arranged by the case which they govern. A number have already been introduced.

Prepositions governing the accusative:

в, во	into	по	up to (many other meanings in set phrases)
за	for (for alternative translations consult dictionary)		
		про	about, concerning
на	on to, on (many other meanings in set phrases)	с, со	about, approximately
		че́рез	over, across, through

Prepositions governing the genitive:

без	without	из	out of, from
вме́сто	instead of	кро́ме	besides
для	for	от	from, away from
до	up to, until, as far as	по́сле	after

про́тив	against	среди́	among
с, со	from, down from	у	at, near, by, in the possession of

Prepositions governing the dative:

к, ко	towards	по	according to, along

Prepositions governing the instrumental:

за	behind, after; for (and other meanings in set phrases)	над	over, above
		под	under
		с, со	with
ме́жду	between		

Prepositions governing the locative:

в, во	in	по	after
на	on (and other meanings in set phrases)	при	with, in the presence (*or* time) of, attached to
о, об, о́бо	about, on		

EXERCISE 9
New words.

всесою́зный	all-Union	связь	connection, link
междуна-ро́дный	international	совеща́ние	conference
		то есть, т.е.	that is, ie
оте́чественный	patriotic	тот, та, то, те	that
предисло́вие	foreword	эпо́ха	epoch, age
ру́копись	manuscript	э́тот, э́та, э́то, э́ти	this

Translate into English.

1. Без цены́, б.ц.
2. До на́ших дней.
3. Исто́рия го́рода за со́рок лет.
4. Из мои́х произведе́ний.

5. К вопро́су о ро́ли (Guess! Nom. is роль) интеллиге́нции (Guess!) в Вели́кой Октя́брьской (Guess!) социалисти́ческой револю́ции.
6. Ме́жду двумя́ война́ми.
7. План вы́пуска литерату́ры на 1972 год.
8. Газе́та на англи́йском языке́.
9. От 5-ого до 2-ого столе́тия до н.э.
10. По Вели́кой Оте́чественной войне́.
11. Под реда́кцией проф. А. П. Боборы́кина.
12. При Петре́ Пе́рвом.
13. Речь про́тив империали́зма Аме́рики.
14. Ле́нин с на́ми!
15. Ле́нин среди́ нас!
16. У неё собра́ние ре́дких ру́кописей.

Key:
1. Without price (unpriced).
2. Up to our [own] days.
3. A [or the] history of the [or a] town for [or over] forty years.
4. From my works.
5. Towards [or on] the question of [or about] the role of the intelligentsia in the Great October Socialist Revolution. (This is the full Soviet title of the October Revolution of 1917: 7th November by the modern calendar.)
6. Between two wars.
7. Plan of issue of literature [ie forthcoming publications] for the year 1972. (Special usage of на with the accusative.)
8. A newspaper in the English language. (Special usage of на with locative.)
9. From the 5th to the 2nd century B.C. (Gen. pl. of столе́тие.)
10. After the Great Patriotic War. (по with locative. The title is the usual Soviet name for the Second World War, or more strictly the war in which the USSR was involved after the German invasion of 22nd June 1941.)
11. Under the editorship of Prof. A. P. Boborykin.
12. In the time of Peter the First (the Great, 1672-1725).
13. A speech against the imperialism of America.
14. Lenin is with us!
15. Lenin is among us!
16. She has (*literally* at her [is]) a collection of rare manuscripts. (This construction with y is a common way of expressing possession where English uses 'to have'.)

1.10. Verbs

1.10.1. Infinitive form
Usually rendered in English as 'to do', 'to see', etc. This is the form in which Russian verbs are entered in dictionaries, and is usually recognizable by the ending -ть, eg читáть 'to read', писáть 'to write'. A few infinitives end in -ти, eg идти́, 'to go'.

1.10.2. Present tense
Most verbs are conjugated with the following pattern of endings:

1st person singular	(I)	-ю or -у
2nd person singular	(you)	-шь
3rd person singular	(he, she, it)	-т
1st person plural	(we)	-м
2nd person plural	(you)	-те
3rd person plural	(they)	-ют or -ут; -ят or ат

Examples:

to read читáть	*to prepare* готóвить	*to go out, be published* вы́йти
я читáю	я готóвлю	я вы́йду
ты читáешь	ты готóвишь	ты вы́йдешь
он, онá, онó читáет	он, онá, онó готóвит	он, онá, онó вы́йдет
мы читáем	мы готóвим	мы вы́йдем
вы читáете	вы готóвите	вы вы́йдете
они́ читáют	они́ готóвят	они́ вы́йдут

Certain verbs undergo consonant changes in some forms of the present tense, eg in писáть 'to write': пишу́, пи́шешь, пи́шет, etc.

1.10.3. Past tense
Russian verbs form their past tense very simply, replacing the -ть ending of the infinitive by the ending -л (masc. sing.), -ла (fem. sing.), -ло (neut. sing.) and -ли (plural), according to the gender and number of their subject, eg:

Masculine: Подготóвил к печáти Н. И. Смúрнов (from подготóвить 'to prepare', ie 'N. I. Smirnov prepared [the work] for [*literally* towards] the press'. The reversal of verb and subject is common in such situations, occurring frequently on title-pages.)

Feminine: Хрестомáтию состáвила Л. Н. Платóнова (from состáвить 'to compile', ie 'L. N. Platonova compiled the collection of readings'. Note the common reversal of subject and object.).

Plural: Журнáлы выходúли ежемéсячно (from выходúть 'to go out, appear, be published', ie 'The journals appeared monthly').

1.10.4. Reflexive verbs

These are usually verbs of which the subject and object refer to the same thing (eg English 'to wash oneself', French 'se laver', German 'sich waschen'). In Russian they assume exactly the same grammatical endings as other verbs, but with the added suffix -ся (-сь after vowels). However, the meaning is not always reflexive. It may be passive, eg

он продолжáет статью́	'he is continuing the article'
статья́ продолжáется	'the article is being continued'
статья́ продолжáлась	'the article was continued'

Other examples are публикýются впервы́е 'are being published for the first time' (публиковáть = 'to publish', hence публиковáться = 'to *be* published'); and готóвятся к вы́пуску 'are being prepared for issue' (готóвить = 'to prepare', hence готóвиться = 'to *be* prepared').

1.10.5. Aspects and the future tense

Most Russian verbs are used in pairs of basic forms, usually similar in appearance. One of these forms, or *aspects*, is normally used to indicate a completed action (the *perfective aspect*), the other to denote an action still in progress (the *imperfective aspect*). For example:

читáть	(ipfve) 'to read, be reading'
прочитáть	(pfve) 'to read, to have read'
я читáл газéту	'I was reading the newspaper'
я прочитáл газéту	'I finished reading the newspaper, read it right through'

Further examples of perfective/imperfective verb pairs:

писа́ть	(ipfve)	} 'to write'
написа́ть	(pfve)	
получа́ть	(ipfve)	} 'to receive'
получи́ть	(pfve)	
выходи́ть	(ipfve)	} 'to go out, be published'
вы́йти	(pfve)	(unrelated basic forms)

Naturally, a perfective verb cannot be used to express a 'present' meaning, and in fact these verbs when used in their 'present' tense forms have a 'future' meaning:

я прочита́ю газе́ту   'I shall read the newspaper'

се́рия вы́йдет в декабре́   'The series will be published in December'

Imperfective verbs may be given a 'future' meaning by using the future tense of быть ('to be'): бу́ду, бу́дешь, etc: он бу́дет писа́ть еженеде́льно 'he will be writing every week

1.10.6. Participles (verbal adjectives)

Two varieties of these adjectives derived from verbs need introduction, the *present participle active* and *past participle passive* (eg English 'collect*ing*' and 'collect*ed*', respectively, from 'to collect'). The participles in Russian are declined like adjectives.

The present participle active is characterized by the adjectival ending -щий, -щая, -щее, etc; eg чита́ющий 'reading', from чита́ть, cf чита́ют 'they read'. Present participles active can also be formed from reflexive verbs, in which case they retain the -ся suffix *after* the ending, which gives them an unfamiliar appearance: продолжа́ющиеся изда́ния 'continuing publications' (from продолжа́ться 'to be continued').

The past participle passive is marked by the adjectival endings -нный, -нная, etc (which are the more frequent) and -тый, -тая, etc. Both sets of endings appear in their short forms when used predicatively:

сле́дующие кни́ги и́зданы не бу́дут 'the following books will not be published' (и́зданы is the 'short' nom. plural form of the past participle passive и́зданный, from изда́ть 'to publish'. Note also the present participle active сле́дующий, from сле́довать 'to follow'.)

кни́га соста́влена коллекти́вом 'the book [is *or* was] compiled by a collective' (соста́влена is the 'short' nom. sing. fem. form of соста́вленный from составля́ть 'to compile'.)

EXERCISE 10

New words (all verbs).

включа́ть (ipfve),	включи́ть (pfve)	to include
выходи́ть (ipfve),	вы́йти (pfve)	to come out, be published
гото́вить (ipfve),	подгото́вить (pfve)	to prepare
издава́ть (ipfve),	изда́ть (pfve)	to publish
писа́ть (ipfve),	написа́ть (pfve)	to write
получа́ть (ipfve),	получи́ть (pfve)	to receive
продолжа́ть (ipfve),	продолжи́ть (pfve)	to continue
публикова́ть (ipfve)		to publish
сле́довать (ipfve)		to follow
составля́ть (ipfve),	соста́вить (pfve)	to compile
чита́ть (ipfve),	прочита́ть (pfve)	to read
явля́ться (ipfve)		to be, serve as (followed by instr.)

Translate into English.

1. В указа́тель включа́ются кни́ги, статьи́ из сбо́рников и продолжа́ющихся изда́ниий, и материа́лы нау́чных конфере́нций.
2. Докла́ды, прочи́танные на пе́рвом сове́тско-америка́нском совеща́нии по свя́зям Се́верной Сиби́ри и Се́верной Аме́рики.
3. Изда́тельство гото́вит к вы́пуску сле́дующие кни́ги.
4. Предисло́вие напи́сано Б. П. Кане́вским.
5. Произведе́ние явля́ется пе́рвым в но́вой се́рии рекоменда́тельных библиогра́фий.

Key:

1. In the index [*or* list] are included books, articles from symposia and serial publications, and materials of scientific conferences. (Reflexive forms of включа́ть, signifying 'to *be* included', and of продолжа́ть, in the form of the present participle active.)
2. Papers read at the first Soviet-American conference on the links between Northern Siberia and North America. (Past participle passive of прочита́ть.)

3. The publishing-house is preparing for publication the following books.
4. The preface [was] written by B. P. Kanevskii. (Past participle passive of написа́ть.)
5. The work is the first in a new series of recommendatory bibliographies. (явля́ться in the sense of 'to be', followed by the instrumental case.)

TRANSLITERATION

Transliteration is, strictly speaking, the use of one alphabet to represent the characters of another. Less strictly, the term is often used as a synonym for 'transcription', to mean the indication of the *sounds* of a language by characters of an alphabet in which it is not customarily written. Since the Roman alphabet normally uses no more than 26 basic characters, and the Cyrillic now used for Russian has 33 characters, the supply of Roman letters has to be eked out with diacritic marks, combinations of letters, or both, in order to achieve an approach to the accurate pronunciation of the Cyrillic original, or a re-transliteration back to Cyrillic.

Another source of confusion is that many of the sounds of Russian which need to be rendered demand varying spellings in the Roman alphabet to make them recognizable and 'pronounceable' in different West European languages. The 'popular' transliterations used, for instance, in newspapers and other non-specialist works, need to put readability before an unambiguous recording of the Cyrillic original. Hence the frequent appearance of the poet Евтушенко as 'Yevtushenko' and 'Jewtuschenko' in many English and German publications respectively, creating a potential source of error in filing or checking an alphabetical list; or French 'Lénine' and English 'Trotsky' to reproduce Ленин and Троцкий. Nor is it uncommon for authors of Russian origin, who have written in Russian, to adopt a simplified or (for example) Anglicized form of name when writing in English. The historian who wrote in English as George Vernadsky, for instance, used a form of name in Russian which could be transliterated Georgii [Vladimirovich] Vernadskii.

2.1. Transliteration from Cyrillic to Roman
Of the many transliteration 'systems' intended to meet the specialist's requirements for accuracy and consistency, the three most often met

with in English-speaking countries are:

1. *The Library of Congress system*, which observes English spelling conventions and is therefore difficult for non-English speakers to follow. It is the most widespread system in US and Canadian library catalogues and bibliographies, and its usage is spreading in the UK, following its employment in the MARC cataloguing service and its adoption by the British Library Reference Division and the *British national bibliography*. It is *not* used by the New York Public Library in the published catalogues (1959 and 1974) of its own extremely rich Slavonic collections, although NYPL adopted the LC system for its current cataloguing from 1972.

2. *The 'British' system of British Standard BS 2979: 1958*, which also follows English spelling conventions, differs from the LC system in its rendering of six Cyrillic characters, only three of which affect filing order. Although now giving some ground to LC, it is still extensively used in the UK, often with its few diacritics omitted. The British Museum and Bodleian Library systems show a few (differing) variations from BS, and both are still in use: the BM system is used for headings in all BM and BLRD printed catalogues published to date, although BLRD has used the LC system for cataloguing its acquisitions from 1971 onwards.

3. *The International Organization for Standards ISO/R9 system*, patterned on the spelling of certain Slavonic languages which do use the Roman alphabet, such as Czech and Croat. It shows a preference for diacritics in contrast to the multi-letter combinations favoured by LC and BS, and differs from the LC system in its rendering of eleven Cyrillic characters, ten of which affect filing order.

The table below takes the LC system as a yardstick, and shows the differences between it and BS, ISO/R9, the NYPL, BM and Bodleian systems, and English, French and German 'popular' variations.

Cyrillic	LC	Variations
а	a	
б	b	
в	v	German often: w
г	g	French sometimes: gu or gh. Occasionally v in -ero, -oro endings

Cyrillic	LC	Variations
д	d	
e	e	NYPL: ye at beginning of word or syllable
ё	ё	Dots often omitted. NYPL usually: io
ж	zh	ISO: ž. French often: j. German often: sh
з	z	German often: s
и	i	
й	ĭ	ISO: j. In BM, final -ий = y, final -ый = uy
к	k	
л	l	
м	m	
н	n	
о	o	
п	p	
р	r	
с	s	German often: ss
т	t	
у	u	French often: ou
ф	f	
х	kh	ISO: h. German and elsewhere often: ch. Sometimes, misleadingly: x
ц	t͡s	Ligature often omitted. BS also omits. ISO: c. NYPL: tz. German often: z
ч	ch	ISO: č. German often: tsch. French often: tch
ш	sh	ISO: š. German often: sch. French often: ch
щ	shch	ISO: šč. German often: schtsch. French often: chtch
ъ	″	Omitted at end of word in LC and most other systems
ы	y	BS strictly: ȳ, but bar usually omitted. BM: ui. Bodleian: î
ь	′	Often omitted in non-specialist transliteration
э	ė	BS: é. BM and Bodleian omit dot

Cyrillic	LC	Variations
ю	i͡u	Ligature often omitted. BS: yu. ISO, German: ju. French: iou
я	i͡a	Ligature often omitted. BS: ya. ISO, German: ja.

(Obsolete characters)

i	i	
ѣ	i͡e	Ligature often omitted. BS, ISO: ê. NYPL: ĕ
ѳ	ḟ	Some systems omit dot
ѵ	ẏ	BS: y̆. BM, Bodleian: i

2.2. Transliteration from Roman to Cyrillic

Russian conventions in transliterating *from* Roman *into* Cyrillic can on occasion cause problems in recognition when English or other non-Russian words appear in a Russian text. In most cases, careful pronunciation as if the word were Russian, and a little imagination, will give the clue. However, below is shown the usual transliteration into Cyrillic of the following English letters:

English	Cyrillic	English	Cyrillic
a	э	l	ль, ie a 'soft' л*
h	г (sometimes х)	unvoiced th	т
j	дж	voiced th	з
		w	у or в

*Russian л alone is pronounced much further back in the throat than in Southern English, closer to the Scottish pronunciation

Thus three English literary figures appear as Вильям Шекспир, Томас Гарди and Джордж Бернард Шо. The western principality becomes Уэльс, and a well-known statesman is transformed into Эдуард Хит (or, less happily, Гит).

In transliteration of French, the many unpronounced letters are omitted, giving, for example, Жан-Жак Руссо. Difficulties with German umlauted vowels result in Йоханн Вольфганг фон Гёте (Goethe) and Мюнхен (München).

Section 3

SOVIET PUBLISHING PRACTICE

This section deals with the organization and internal practices of the present-day Soviet publishing industry and book trade, concentrating on those features which are most likely to concern librarians handling Soviet publications.

In terms of output (in millions of copies), the Soviet publishing industry is certainly one of the two largest in the world: arguments about whether it is or is not larger than that of the USA remain inconclusive, but about 80,000 book and pamphlet titles have been appearing annually in the USSR for the past decade. The widely accepted Western picture of Soviet publishing is one of a vast and monolithic organization responding faithfully to every kink in the Party line as it emanates from the Kremlin. This is an over-simplification of the real position because, although Soviet publishing *is* subject to a much higher degree of central administrative and political control than is usual in Western Europe and North America, areas of authority in the publishing field overlap and in some degree conflict, and some scope for initiative still lies with individual publishing-houses and writers.

However, it remains true that the publishing of books, journals and newspapers is regarded by the Soviet authorities as a very important sector of the mass media, and as a social, political and cultural undertaking which deserves support (including considerable funds) from the state. A proviso, of course, is that the publishing industry should produce material of which the Soviet state and the Communist Party approve as being suitable for Soviet citizens to read. The Communist Party apparatus, which functions in many respects as a separate administration in guiding and checking on the work of government departments, tries to ensure that this is what happens by maintaining a standing watch on publishing policy. The Party's Department of Propaganda keeps in close touch with the State Committee for Publishing, Printing and the Book Trade (*Goskomizdat*), which is effectively a ministry that acts as the main planning and supervisory organ for the book, journal and newspaper industry.

The State Committee for Publishing heads a hierarchy of subordinate local publishing administrations throughout the Soviet Union, and it is this network of government offices which oversees the work of most individual publishing-houses. The so-called 'central' publishers (that is, most of the larger and more important houses in Moscow and Leningrad) are supervised directly by the central offices of the State Committee for Publishing in Moscow, while publishers in Kiev, for example, are answerable to the State Committee's subordinate administration in the Ukraine. In each case this 'superior organ' will review, amend and approve each house's publishing plans, will keep an eye on its financial position, and will try to enforce a massive corpus of regulations and instructions about the way in which the house conducts its affairs.

A small number of publishing-houses are not under the direct authority of the State Committee for Publishing but are answerable to some other body. For example, the Academy of Sciences of the USSR supervises the 'Nauka' publishing-house, and other houses are run by the Party itself, the Writers' Union of the USSR and certain other organizations. However, permission to set up a new publishing-house — of whatever subordination — can only be given at high level by the Party authorities, and is in fact granted only rarely. Soviet policy is strongly against the proliferation of publishing outlets, both for the sake of tighter control and to avoid the penalties of duplication, and this is why Soviet publishing-houses are so few in number: just over 200 in 1980, compared with at least double that number in the UK.

Publishing-houses proper account for about 95% of book and pamphlet *copies* issued in the USSR, but for only about half the number of *titles* appearing each year. The reason is that, besides the publishing-houses themselves, there are several hundred other organizations (research institutes, government departments, educational organs, scientific information centres and so on) which have the right to issue certain sorts of printed matter; and, as the figures suggest, they produce many titles with a very low average number of copies per title. Material of this kind is rarely available through the book trade, and presents a serious acquisition problem to the librarian outside, and even inside, the Soviet Union. The same applies in the field of journal publishing: most regular journals are issued by officially constituted publishing-houses, but many other organizations produce serial publications in a sporadic (even haphazard) manner. Repeated campaigns by the authorities to bring more control — both bibliographical and otherwise — into this area of non-trade publishing have so far had only limited success.

If we trace the progress of a work written by a Soviet author from the manuscript stage to publication, a number of other special features in the Soviet publishing system become apparent. As in Western publishing practice, most manuscripts submitted to a publisher are either sent in on the author's own initiative, or are commissioned by the publishing-house from an author under a contract. However, Soviet publishers are also liable to be instructed by their 'superior organ' to publish certain works (although the frequency of such instructions varies with the type of publisher), and they will also receive a good deal of guidance and recommendation over the emphasis to be given in their publishing plans to different topics and styles of treatment. In the case of an unsolicited manuscript, the process of selection and rejection is done largely by the publishers' own editorial staff, in the light of the work's quality, the appropriateness of its subject to the house's own specialization and, of course, its likely political acceptability.

Each manuscript accepted for publication is placed under the supervision of an editor on the publisher's staff, called a *vedushchii redaktor*, who checks it in detail with the author to decide on possible alterations, supervises its production, and monitors its sales and public reception. She will usually be assisted by a 'design editor' (*khudozhestvennyi redaktor*) and a 'technical editor' (*tekhnicheskii redaktor*), and the names of all these editors will appear on the last printed page of the work (a practice originally decreed by Lenin in order to establish personal responsibility in the event of special praise or blame attaching to the book subsequently). These editors must be distinguished, of course, from those editors or editorial committees who are responsible for selecting articles for inclusion in a collection of papers (a *sbornik* — a very common form of Soviet scholarly publication), and also from editorial boards which plan and supervise the compilation of large publications such as major reference works. These are often eminent scholars or specialists in their own field, and not normally publishing-house staff.

Before permission is given for printing to begin, the publisher must send brief details of the work, including a summary of its subject matter, to the State Committee for Publishing in Moscow. Staff there will run the data through a computer-based system to check for any duplication with other publishers' proposals, and will also give a preliminary verdict on the work's desirability from the viewpoint of the overall pattern of publishing and current political lines. If the work is approved by the State Committee, it can then be incorporated into the house's publication plans, and will in due course figure in the annual plan (*templan*) of forthcoming publications, which will be widely distributed to the Soviet book trade, and to the book export organization Mezhdunarodnaya Kniga for selective inclusion in their weekly list *Novye knigi SSSR*. The book trade organizations are expected to submit to the publisher a statement of the number of copies they require of each title, well before the beginning of the planned year of publication (except in the case of export orders), and these figures are the basis for decisions on the number of copies to be printed of each title.

However, an important constraint on the decision over the edition size is the amount of paper allocated to the publisher each year. The USSR has had for many years, and still has, a severe shortage of paper for printing, and it is more usual than not for the edition size of a book to be cut to well below the level which would satisfy all the pre-publication orders placed for it: hence the phenomenon of many Soviet books becoming 'out of print' immediately upon publication. The Soviet publishing-house does not depend on retail sales for its economic survival to the same crucial extent as a Western publisher. Most of its output is disposed of to the wholesale book trade organizations under a firm contract agreed before publication, and not on a sale-or-return basis. So, even if the Soviet publisher has insufficient paper to meet the demand for a particular title, at least he knows fairly accurately, before the work appears in the bookshops, how much income he will derive from it. He cannot, however, manipulate the *price* of a book to influence the size of the market or to increase his profits. Book prices in the Soviet Union must be calculated according to government-approved scales which take into account the type of publication, its intended readership and its length, but not the financial state of individual publishing-houses. If, in the event, the prices which a publishing-house has to charge make it impossible for overall outlay to be covered, the state will provide a subsidy to ensure that the house continues to issue works which the authorities think desirable at prices which are felt to be appropriate. In practice, this means that the prices of most school textbooks, for example, are heavily subsidized, as are the prices of many books in non-Russian languages issued for the smaller national minorities.

Returning to the progress of our typical manuscript: once approval has been secured from the State Committee for Publishing, the manuscript will be sent to the printer for setting, and a small number of copies will be run off as galley proofs. When these have been proofread by the author and a staff proofreader, they are passed to the censorship office. The main censorship organ (usually called *Glavlit*) maintains staff on the premises of each publishing-house, and they are responsible for the detailed scrutiny of all printed matter at the galley-proof, and subsequently the page-proof stages, checking both specifically for any mention of 'official secrets' and in general for the observation of current political lines and nuances. Only after the *Glavlit* official has issued a certificate passing the book for distribution can the main print run begin. (The number of the censor's certificate is usually printed on the last page of the book.)

Where the edition size falls below the total number of copies ordered, distribution to wholesale agencies within the USSR is supposed to be made on the basis of a set ratio of copies supplied to copies ordered, depending on the extent of the shortfall. Export orders receive priority in this respect, and genuine – though not always successful – efforts are made to meet advance orders from abroad in full. Many non-periodical works intended for wide circulation are published in a series and are available only under a standing order or 'subscription' (*podpiska*), both within the USSR and abroad. Some editions are reserved exclusively for Soviet libraries, in an attempt to make the copies printed as widely accessible to the general public as possible. At the other end of the scale, some highly specialized technical, scientific and scholarly works have their print run set to correspond solely to the advance orders received, and are supplied to meet those orders only. All these limitations have combined to create a lively market in the USSR for the sale and exchange of second-hand publications – some of it conducted officially through bookshops, but with the rest of the market shading (in the eyes of the authorities) from grey to black in cases where very high prices can be asked and obtained.

Further reading
The standard work in English on Soviet publishing up to the late 1950s is:

Gorokhoff, Boris I. *Publishing in the USSR.* (Slavic and East European series, 19.) Bloomington, Indiana UP, 1959. 306 pp.

A more recent treatment, emphasizing the contemporary organization of the Soviet publishing industry, is:

Walker, Gregory. *Soviet book publishing policy*. Cambridge UP, 1978. xv, 164 pp.

An informative presentation of accepted Soviet views on the development and present state of publishing in the USSR is:

Puzikov, A., Likhtenshtein, Y. & Sikorsky, N. *Books in the USSR*. Moscow, Iskusstvo/Progress, 1975. 95 pp., numerous illus.

Section 4

NOTES ON ACQUISITION AND INTERLENDING

Difficulties in the acquisition of material in Russian arise for several reasons: the speed with which many Soviet titles become, in practice, 'out of print'; the limited number of dealers outside the USSR with adequate stocks and expertise in handling Soviet titles, and the impossibility of ordering commercially direct from the Soviet Union; the delays and uncertainties often associated with exchange agreements; the scarcity and high prices of out-of-print material in Russian; and the variety of alternatives to an original copy, thanks to microform and reprint publishing.

The most reliable method of obtaining new Soviet publications is, not surprisingly, to order in advance of publication from an experienced supplier — whether a dealer or an exchange partner. For comment on *Novye knigi SSSR* as a source of advance information, see 6.1.3. The annual publishing plans of some Soviet publishing-houses are distributed in limited numbers outside the USSR. The titles they forecast will not all appear in *NK*, and they have the advantage of showing an entire year's publishing programme, subject though this will be to modifications, delays and cancellations. 'Nauka', the largest Soviet scholarly publisher, has begun to list its titles for 1983 onwards in quarterly plans, except for works issued by its offices for physical-mathematical and for Oriental literature, which will continue to be covered by annual plans. All titles should be listed in *NK*.

Periodicals available on subscription to customers outside the USSR (again via dealers or exchange partners) are listed in an annual catalogue, *Gazety i zhurnaly SSSR* (English title: *Periodicals of the USSR*). Subscriptions should be placed well in advance of the desired commencement date to secure a complete run of issues: suppliers will advise on the appropriate period. Missing issues and back runs of Soviet serials are very difficult to obtain commercially, but are sometimes to be had through exchange partners.

56

Acquiring titles even recently published can often require speculative approaches to several suppliers. See 6.1.1. and 6.1.4. for comment on *Knizhnaya letopis'* and *Knizhnoe obozrenie* as sources of information on recent Soviet publications. The older the item, the smaller the number of copies printed, the more remote its place of publication, and the less acceptable its political standpoint in the USSR of today, the more probable it becomes that one will need to be satisfied with something other than an original copy.

It will be found that some titles are reported as 'not available for export'. This applies in particular to unpriced publications (marked б.ц. or беспл. in *Knizhnaya letopis'* and бесплатно on the back cover). Since 1982, most other Soviet publications cannot be sent or taken out of the USSR except through official channels (eg under an exchange agreement) or with the written permission of the appropriate Soviet authorities and after payment of customs duty. Those visiting the Soviet Union should carefully check the regulations in force before attempting to post or otherwise export Soviet publications from the country.

4.1. Purchase

When considering purchase and subscription for Russian publications from the British, European and American book trade, it should be borne in mind that a relatively small number of dealers have wide experience of trading in Russian and Soviet material. Even fewer are permitted by the Soviet book export organization, 'Mezhdunarodnaya Kniga', to deal with it direct in ordering new Soviet publications. Prices charged by dealers for new Soviet books will usually be appreciably higher than a direct conversion of prices given in *Novye knigi SSSR* would suggest. This is partly because books are often published at a higher price than that quoted in *NK*, which is only intended to be approximate; but besides this, 'Mezhdunarodnaya Kniga' includes a percentage surcharge in its price to dealers. Beyond this point, each dealer will have his own practice with respect to profit margins.

The list below shows firms known to handle Russian and Soviet material regularly, although not all of them deal exclusively in such publications. Comments in brackets reflect recent experience of their services as in late 1982, but absence of comment does not necessarily imply an adverse opinion.

Great Britain

Blackwell's, 48/51 Broad Street, Oxford OX1 3BQ. 0865 249111,
   244944. (Russian language and literature.)

K. J. Bredon's Bookshop, 70 East Street, Brighton BN1 1HP.
   0273 29536.

Central Books Ltd, 37 Grays Inn Road, London WC1X 8PS.
   01-242 6166. (Especially for Soviet books in English.)

Collets Holdings Ltd, Denington Estate, Wellingborough, Northants
   NN8 2QT. 0933 224531. (MK's agent for the UK. Extensive stock
   of recent Soviet publications. Use this address for periodical subscriptions and library orders.)

Collets International Bookshop, 129-131 Charing Cross Road, London
   WC2 0EQ. 01-734 0782/3. (Shop and retail sales.)

H. Fellner, 70 Gascony Avenue, London NW6 4NE. 01-624 5417.

Flegon Press, 37B New Cavendish Street, London W1M 3JR.

W. Forster, 83A Stamford Hill, London N16 5TP. 01-800 3919.

W. & G. Foyle Ltd, 119 Charing Cross Road, London WC2.
   01-437 5660.

Anthony C. Hall, 30 Staines Road, Twickenham TW2 5AH.
   01-898 2638. (Large second-hand stock on and from Russia and
   Eastern Europe.)

Hammersmith Books, Lifford's Place, Barnes High Street, London
   SW13. 01-876 7254.

Holdan Books, 15 North Parade Avenue, Oxford OX2 6XL.
   0865 57971. (Emigré and Western material, also recent Soviet publications, especially in language and literature.)

Ben Kane Book Service, 33 Kenver Avenue, London N12 0PG.
   01-445 5623.

R. W. Malynowsky, 18 Doughty Street, London WC1N 2PL.

Europe and Israel

Akateeminen Kirjakauppa, Postilokero 128, 00101 Helsinki 10, Finland.

Le Bibliophile Russe, 12 rue Lamartine, 75009 Paris, France. (Second-
   hand and antiquarian, especially émigré Russian.)

Brücken-Verlag GmbH, Ackerstrasse 3, 4000 Düsseldorf 1, Federal
   Republic of Germany. (Chiefly recent Soviet books.)

Bukinist, POB 153, Ramat-Gan, Israel. (Second-hand and antiquarian.)

I. Chmeljuk, 1 rue de Fleurus, 75006, Paris, France.

Les Editeurs Réunis, 11 rue de la Montagne-Ste-Geneviève, 75005 Paris, France. (Emigré and Western books in Russian, also second-hand and antiquarian from the USSR.)

Journalfranz Arnulf Liebing GmbH, Postfach 1136, 87 Würzburg 2, Federal Republic of Germany. (Recent and older Soviet publications, mostly from Soviet libraries' exchange stocks; also reprints.)

M. Kipnis, POB 4042, Tel-Aviv, Israel.

Kubon und Sagner, PO Box 34 01 08, D-8000 München 34, Federal Republic of Germany. (Very wide range of new and older Russian and Soviet books.)

Les Livres Etrangers SA, 10 rue Armand Moisant, 75737 Paris Cedex 15, France. (MK's agent in France. Large stock of recent Soviet publications. Excellent standing order and subscription service.)

A. Neimanis Buchvertrieb GmbH, Bauerstrasse 28, 8000 München 40, Federal Republic of Germany. (Emigré and Western publications in Russian.)

E. Neustein, 94 Allenby, POB 29443, Tel Aviv, Israel.

Martinus Nijhoff BV, Lange Voorhout 9-11, POB 269, The Hague, Netherlands. (Antiquarian.)

Saint-Pétersbourg SARL, 106 rue de Miromesnil, 75008 Paris, France. (Second-hand and antiquarian, especially émigré Russian.)

Wilh. Smolders, POB 29, A-1162 Vienna, Austria. (Antiquarian.)

Alexander Timofejeff, CP 630, I-00100 Roma-Centro, Italy. (Second-hand and émigré publications. Agent of Possev-Verlag.)

Jacob Tversky, 20 Shenkin St, Tel-Aviv 65 231, PO Box 4356, Israel. (Second-hand and antiquarian.)

Zentralantiquariat der DDR, Talstrasse 29, 701 Leipzig, German Democratic Republic. (Second-hand and older Soviet and Russian books; also reprints.)

United States

Ardis Russian Book Distribution, 2901 Heatherway, Ann Arbor, Michigan 48104, USA.

Four Continents Book Corporation, 149 Fifth Avenue, New York, NY 10010, USA.

Victor Kamkin, 12224 Parklawn Drive, Rockville, Maryland 20852, USA. (Probably the largest dealer in Russian books in the US.)

Philip Lozinski, 1504 Drift Road, Westport, Massachusetts 02790, USA.

Russica Book and Art Shop, Inc, 799 Broadway, New York, NY 10003, USA. (New and older Soviet and émigré Russian publications.)

George Sabo Slavic Books, 23 Stuyvesant Place, Elberon, New Jersey 07740, USA. (Second-hand and antiquarian Russian and other East European books.)

Szwede Books, POB 1214, Palo Alto, California 94302, USA.

4.2. Exchanges

Exchanges with libraries and other institutions in the USSR are useful sources of supply under certain circumstances only. Libraries requiring only a limited number of Soviet books and journals, which are recent titles from major publishing-houses, would normally find a reliable commercial dealer preferable to exchanges as a means of acquisition. Exchange partners vary greatly in enthusiasm and reliability, although most of the larger Soviet libraries are well used to exchange transactions. Some partners can be invaluable in procuring out-of-print books, back runs of serials, irregular series and small-edition non-commercial publications which are unobtainable in the original through other channels. Many can also supply microfilms of material not otherwise available. The two types of Western library likely to benefit most from exchanges are, firstly, the large library requiring older or more obscure publications on an appreciable scale and with the budget to afford them: it is easier for large libraries to bear the fluctuating financial demands of an exchange agreement. Secondly, the highly specialized library may be able to find similarly specialized partners with access to material hard to acquire commercially − particularly if the 'home' library can offer desirable publications of its own.

Exchanges on a 'value-for-value' basis are usually acceptable to Soviet libraries, but they prefer a title-for-title or volume-for-volume basis if the partner is willing. It is common to find a supplementary charge added to the rouble price of an item for exchange valuation purposes, and a few Soviet libraries fix special 'exchange' prices even for recent publications at figures far higher than the original published price in the USSR. Such practices, together with the extra administrative costs of operating exchanges, must be taken into account in deciding whether to conclude an exchange agreement. It is also important to reach a clear understanding over the range of material which the prospective partner is in a position to supply, and to insist − where necessary − that unsolicited items should not be sent.

Some Soviet libraries are willing to conclude 'blanket order' agreements, under which they will supply on exchange all titles available to them (*not* necessarily all titles published) in categories specified by their partner. Such arrangements should not be regarded as guaranteeing comprehensive coverage of the categories concerned, and the financial commitment they incur should be carefully monitored. Many libraries can supply only the publications of their own institution or locality, or items from a limited 'exchange collection' (*obmennyi fond*). Very naturally, they will offer the more attractive material, and more favourable terms, to foreign partners who are willing to respond to their most urgent needs, and who conduct their exchanges in a friendly and cooperative spirit, especially when this can be reinforced by personal contact. Letters in English to Soviet libraries are normally understood, if they are clearly and simply expressed (although letters in good Russian will be much appreciated); but many Soviet libraries prefer to send all their own correspondence in Russian.

4.3. Reprints and microforms

Many publishers are now issuing books and journals in Russian in one or other of these forms of reproduction. Concentration has tended to be on large reference and bibliographical works, back runs of scholarly and literary journals, and treatises of recognized academic worth. Some publishers have embarked on very large copying projects (eg of Russian and Soviet legal materials, and of Russian books from the eighteenth century), in some cases using the resources of Soviet libraries. There is at present no published up-to-date guide to commercial reproductions of Russian-language material, but the Slavonic and East European Branch of the British Library Reference Division (Great Russell Street, London WC1B 3DG) maintains a Central Cyrillic Reprint Register, intended to record all such reproductions, both full-size and microform, and will answer enquiries about the availability of specific titles. The annuals *Guide to microforms in print* and *Guide to reprints* include the output of most microform and reprint publishers, respectively, and publishers' own prospectuses can, of course, be obtained. Those with substantial listings of Russian titles include:

Bell & Howell Micro Photo Division, Old Mansfield Road, Wooster,
   Ohio 44691, USA, *and* Telford Road, Bicester, Oxon OX6 0UP,
   England.

Datamatics Inc, 120 Liberty Street, New York, NY 10006, USA.

Europe Printing Establishment, POB 184, FL-9490 Vaduz, Liechtenstein.

General Microfilm Company, 70 Coolidge Hill Road, Watertown,
Massachusetts 02172, USA.

Inter-Documentation AG, Poststrasse 14, 6300 Zug, Switzerland.

KTO Microform, FL-9491 Nendeln, Liechtenstein.

Nauka Ltd, 2-30-19 Minami-Ikebukuro, Toshima-ku, Tokyo 171,
Japan.

Oriental Research Partners, POB 158, Newtonville, Massachusetts
02160, USA.

Readex Microprint Corp, 101 Fifth Avenue, New York, NY 10003,
USA, *and* Readex Microprint Ltd, 48 Bloomsbury Street, London
WC1B 3QT.

Russia Micro-Project, Killan Library, Dalhousie University, Halifax,
Nova Scotia B3H 4H8, Canada.

University Microfilms International, 300 North Zeeb Road, Ann Arbor,
Michigan 48106, USA, *and* 18 Bedford Row, London WC1R 4EJ.

Zentralantiquariat der DDR, Reprint-Abteilung, PSF 1080, Talstrasse
29, DDR-701 Leipzig, German Democratic Republic.

Most Western European and North American libraries will be willing to
supply, for a charge and subject to copyright restrictions, microfilms
or photocopies of Russian (or other) publications in their collections.
Some publish lists of works available in microform from their stocks.
On copyright, see 4.6. below.

4.4. Duplicates from other libraries
Most libraries collecting material in Russian acquire duplicates over the
years (chiefly owing to the identification difficulties dealt with in 5.3
and 5.13!). Few have time to prepare and circulate lists, but many will
be happy for a visitor to make his selection on the spot. Disposal may
be for cost of delivery only, at some proportion of the original cost, or
by exchange.

4.5. Inter-library loans
For books and journals in Russian, the primary inter-lending source in
the United Kingdom is the British Library Lending Division at Boston

Spa. BLLD holds a very extensive Russian-language stock of its own, especially of current Soviet journals in all subjects, and of Soviet scientific and technical non-serials; and its Slavonic Union Catalogue records a fairly high proportion of Russian publications held in other British lending libraries. It does not include the holdings of the BL's Reference Division. Loan requests for Russian material can also be forwarded by BLLD to libraries abroad, including those in the USSR. A wide range of material can now be obtained on loan from the Soviet Union, although there are currently (1982) prohibitions on the loan of many individual items and certain categories of publication, including Soviet dissertations. Soviet and other East European libraries will normally deal only with loan requests sent through a national centre such as BLLD, but many libraries in Western Europe and the USA will consider applications direct from the requesting library. Some Western libraries with rich holdings of Russian and Soviet material will not lend, however, and the requesting library may have to purchase a microfilm or xerox copy of the work needed.

Scrupulous accuracy in transliteration, and completeness of bibliographical detail, are both essential in formulating inter-library loan requests for publications in Russian. Garbled spelling or the omission of data (especially of any element which might serve as a heading) can easily cause a search to fail. A photocopy of the original reference is required by BLLD, and is recommended for other requests. By the same token, in checking Russian loan requests received by one's own library, it is necessary to be alive to the possibility of confused spellings, different transliteration conventions, and alternative catalogue headings.

4.6. Copyright restrictions

A library may well consider commissioning its own microfilm or photocopy of a Russian-language work held in, or borrowed from, another collection. However, it must be borne in mind that the USSR acceded to the Universal Copyright Convention on 27th May 1973, and that the reproduction of works published in the Soviet Union from that date onwards is subject to the usual restrictions laid down by copyright legislation in the copying library's own country. The same restrictions will apply to the copying of works in Russian published outside the USSR (in, for example, the USA, France, the Federal Republic of Germany or the UK); but publications which appeared in the Soviet

Union before the date of its accession to the Universal Copyright Convention may be copied without limitation. It should be noted that microfilms and reprints of pre-1973 Soviet publications produced by Western organizations may be protected from further reproduction by copyright statements inserted at the beginning of the film or volume.

Further reading

Useful papers on exchanges and inter-library lending with the USSR are contained in: 'Anglo-Soviet conference on library cooperation', *Interlending review*, 7(2), 1979, pp. 52-56, and supplement of full text of selected papers on 6 microfiches.

See also Vaclav Laska's article 'Acquisition of current material from Eastern Europe', in: Samore, T., comp. and ed., *Acquisition of foreign materials for US libraries*, 2nd ed. (Metuchen/London, Scarecrow Press, 1982), pp. 118-124. This updates but does not fully supersede Laska's article at pp. 195-203 in the first edition of the same work (Scarecrow Press, 1973).

As guides to the location of Russian and other Slavonic materials in libraries, the following directories can be consulted:

Walker, Gregory, ed. *Resources for Soviet, East European and Slavonic studies in British libraries.* Birmingham Univ., Centre for Russian and East European Studies, 1981. 240 pp.

Lewanski, Richard C. *Eastern Europe and Russia/Soviet Union. A handbook of West European archival and library resources.* NY etc, K. G. Saur, 1980. xv, 317 pp.

Grant, Stephen A. *Scholar's guide to Washington DC for Russian/ Soviet area studies.* Washington, Smithsonian Inst. Press, 1977. 404 pp.

Teich, Gerhard. *Topographie der Osteuropa-, Südosteuropa- und DDR-Sammlungen.* München/NY, Verlag Dokumentation, 1978. 388 pp.

Section 5

NOTES ON CATALOGUING

The cataloguing of material in Russian presents certain special problems arising from the language, the Cyrillic alphabet, the conditions under which Soviet works are written and published, and Soviet conventions in book design and production. Some of the more commonly occurring difficulties are considered here. 'AACR2' references are to the *Anglo-American cataloguing rules. Second edition* of 1978.

5.1. Language and transliteration

Unless a separate Cyrillic file is maintained in the order of the Cyrillic alphabet, catalogue entries for works in Russian will require at least a transliterated heading for filing purposes. Whether the body of the entry is given in Cyrillic or transliterated — Romanized, in the AACR terminology — will depend on the importance attached to preservation of the original, the availability and cost of Cyrillic typing or printing facilities, and any limitations imposed by machine-readable records. (The Library of Congress decided in 1979 to transliterate the full text of Cyrillic entries, allowing their incorporation into the MARC database.)

5.2. Authors and compilers

A bibliographical distinction between the Russian words áвтор ('author') and составитель ('compiler') is not always clearly drawn. A 'compiler' may be mentioned only on the verso of the title-page in a Russian book, but appear in the 'author's' position in the colophon (see 5.12) and as an 'author' heading in the national bibliography.

5.3. Authors and editors

Many Soviet publications are written by a number of authors in collaboration, and/or edited by a group acting as a редакционная коллегия ('editorial board'). Where this occurs, the correct catalogue heading to be allotted under some Western conventions may be in doubt, and there is a danger of the entry's receiving a heading untraceable in Soviet bibliographies and unfindable from data given in Soviet references. The degree of responsibility for a work exercised by an editor (редактор), a 'responsible editor' (ответственный редактор), or even a 'chief editor' (главный редактор), varies greatly, and this, together with the number of 'editors' of various kinds often involved with a single work (see Section 3), may result in a variety of interpretations of the relevant cataloguing rules and hence of headings allotted. AACR2, however, is in general agreement with Soviet bibliographical practice in preferring the title as main heading where personal authorship is unknown or diffuse, or when the work is a collection or produced under editorial direction (AACR2, 21.1C). The colophon (see 5.12), or the facsimile catalogue entry now often printed in Soviet books, will usually indicate the main heading which a work will receive in Soviet bibliographies.

5.4. Institutional responsibility

It is common practice for Soviet scholarly and educational works to carry at the head of their title-page the name of the institution under whose auspices the book has been produced, or the name of the ministry or department which has approved its use. The mention of this institution on a title-page does not normally, however, imply that it has the degree of responsibility for a work's appearance which would justify the use of its name as a catalogue heading. Exceptions are usually fairly obvious, notably reports, proceedings, statutes, regulations, etc, produced by government and Party organizations and other bodies in pursuit of their official functions. AACR2, 21.1B2, lays down the presumption that a corporate body's title should not be used as a heading unless the publication falls clearly into certain specified categories of this kind.

It should be noted that many Soviet institutions carry within their full name a statement of any important award or honour they have received, and many more are named after an individual or body. To avoid over-long wording, many Western catalogues and bibliographies dispense with either or both of these elements where no confusion can ensue. An example of both practices is the Госуда́рственная о́рдена Ле́нина библиоте́ка СССР и́мени В. И. Ле́нина ('State Order of Lenin Library of the USSR named after V. I. Lenin'). Soviet usage will sometimes dispense with the wording of the Order, but never with the 'named after' element if the person concerned is Lenin, and only rarely in the case of others. AACR2, 24.5B, states that honours and orders should be omitted from institutional titles used as headings.

5.5. Full personal names

The full personal name of a Soviet author, including forename, patronymic and surname (see 1.6), is usually shown only in the colophon (see 5.12), not on the title-page. Even in the colophon, the full name is only given for the author or authors directly responsible for writing the book. Editors, and contributors to collective works, are normally given initials only. Current Soviet bibliographies show initials, or occasionally forename only.

5.6. Grammatical form of name

Personal names requiring inclusion in the catalogue entry may appear in a variety of grammatical forms which need to be recognized and sometimes converted to follow cataloguing conventions. Note particularly that:

the *genitive* case will appear after под ред. ('under the editorship of . . .') and similar phrases. The author's name may also appear in the genitive immediately after the title, eg 'Война́ и мир' Л. Н. Толсто́го ('War and Peace' by L. N. Tolstoi).

the *dative* case will appear in formulae of presentation in Festschriften and the like, eg П. А. Па́влову к 75-ле́тию со дня рожде́ния ('*to* P. A. Pavlov on the occasion of his 75th birthday').

the *instrumental* case will appear after past participles such as сост. [а́влен] ('compiled *by*').

the *plural* form is used where two authors have the same surname, as in the case of spouses or brothers, eg Е. и М. Нико́льские (nom. pl. of Нико́льский, Нико́льская).

All personal names in headings are converted to the *nominative* case. For declensions see 1.6, and for a quick-recognition table of endings see 8.1.

5.7. State and Party names as headings

The variety of catalogue headings used in Western libraries for the territory now covered by the Soviet Union, or for its government, has been brought about by the complex history of the country's official designations. 'Russia' was the name normally applied in English (as was Россия in Russian) to the Russian Empire (Российская Импéрия) ruled by the tsars, and to the territory controlled by their immediate successors, the Provisional Government of February to October 1917. After the October Revolution of 1917, the Bolshevik government proclaimed in January 1918 the Russian Soviet Federated Socialist Republic (RSFSR) (Российская Совéтская Федератúвная Социалистúческая Респýблика), as the title of the state which was ruled from Moscow and which de facto excluded many of the peripheral areas of the former Russian Empire in which independence had been proclaimed or where civil was was still in progress (eg Finland, Poland, the Ukraine, the Caucasus, Central Asia and Eastern Siberia). The ending of the civil war and the extension of Bolshevik control enabled the formation in December 1922 of the Union of Soviet Socialist Republics or USSR (Сою́з Совéтских Социалистúческих Респýблик — СССР) as a state comprising the RSFSR and three other 'soviet socialist republics'. Further republics were subsequently added to and subtracted from the Union, before the present composition was reached, consisting of 15 'union republics', and 20 'autonomous republics' of lower constitutional status. The RSFSR (often called the Russian Federation — Российская Федерáция) remains by far the largest of the 15 union republics, but is constitutionally on a level with the rest, such as the Ukrainian or the Kazakh SSRs. Like the other union republics, it maintains a range of ministries and other official organs quite distinct from the 'all-Union' ministries and departments whose responsibilities extend over the entire Soviet Union.

According to modern Anglo-American cataloguing practice (AACR2, 23.2A and 23.3), the heading used for the state should be the English form, where in use, of the name applicable at the time of publication (eg 'Union of Soviet Socialist Republics' for the Soviet state from 30th December 1922 onwards). The practice of many major British and

American libraries, however, has been to use 'Russia' as the heading even when applied to publications of the Soviet period, sometimes followed by a series of subheadings to indicate changes of official title or jurisdiction. This convention is to be found in the catalogues of the Library of Congress (including the Slavic Cyrillic Union Catalog), the New York Public Library, and the British Museum Library and British Library Reference Division.

The Communist Party of the Soviet Union is *not* formally an organ of the Soviet government, despite its leading role in Soviet society, and should not appear as a subheading following the headings 'USSR' or 'Russia' (despite the usage found in the catalogues of the British Museum Library and BLRD, where CPSU publications are included under 'Russia — miscellaneous institutions, societies, etc'). The Party's title has changed as frequently as that of its home country, as follows:

1898-1918   Российская социал-демократическая рабочая партия (РСДРП). In 1917, (большевиков), 'of the Bolsheviks', was added in brackets, reflecting the long-standing split dividing the RSDRP into majority (Bolshevik) and minority (Menshevik) factions.

1918-1925   Российская коммунистическая партия (большевиков) — РКП(б).

1925-1952   Всесоюзная коммунистическая партия (большевиков) — ВКП(б).

1952-   Коммунистическая партия Советского Союза — КПСС.

5.8. Names of non-Russian origin

Authors of non-Russian origin writing in Russian may appear in headings under the 'native' form of their name, or in a transliteration of the Russian rendering of that native form, eg Herzen *or* Gertsen (from Герцен), Baudouin de Courtenay *or* Boduėn de Kurtenė (from Бодуэн де Куртенэ). Decisions in individual cases will depend partly on treatment of the name in reference sources, where it may have become regarded as Russianized (eg Kyukhel'beker, from Кюхельбекер, rather than Küchelbäcker), and partly on the frequency of the author's writings in the language of his 'native' name, if any.

5.9. Edition statements

The Russian word изда́ние may need to be rendered in English by either 'edition' or 'impression', since второе (etc) изда́ние may be applied as readily to an unchanged reissue as to a radically altered or much-expanded fresh edition. Тира́ж, used in this context, is always equivalent to 'impression'. Explanatory wording is commonly added to the edition statement on the title-page, and will usually clarify the position.

Examples:

3-е изда́ние, допо́лненное	'3rd, supplemented *edition*'
2-е изда́ние, расши́ренное	'2nd, expanded *edition*'
4-е изда́ние, перерабо́танное	'4th, re-worked *edition*'
10-е изда́ние, стереоти́пное	'10th, stereotyped [ie unchanged] *impression*'
дополни́тельный тира́ж	'additional *impression*'

5.10. Imprint

Note the standard Russian bibliographical abbreviations for towns most frequently occurring as places of publication:

Л. Ленингра́д (1924-   )
М. Москва́
П., Пг. Петрогра́д (1914-24)
Спб. Санктпетербу́ргъ (to 1914)

5.11. Volume statement

It is common for the first, or even the first few, volumes in a Soviet published series, especially if irregular, to bear no volume numbering on the title-page or cover, and the relationship between volumes may have to be deduced from similarities of title and/or statements printed in the introduction to one or more of the volumes.

The number of volumes in a multi-volume set is often stated in the form of a sub-title, eg в трёх тома́х ('in three volumes'). Inclusion of this statement in a catalogue entry can be useful both as a differentiation between editions and as an indication of progress in publishing an uncompleted set.

Note that кни́га and часть (as in в двух кни́гах, часть пе́рвая/втора́я) may be used as well as том as the unit for volume numbering, whether the volumes are physically separate or not. Where a multi-volume work is further subdivided, том, книга and часть are usually used in that (descending) order, eg том II, кн. 2, часть тре́тья. Вы́пуск ('issue') may also be translatable as 'volume', but normally denotes a serial or other work issued in parts over time. Но́мер ('issue' or 'number') also bears this latter sense, with reference to periodicals and newspapers only.

5.12. Colophons

A colophon, or 'publishing particulars', is obliged by law to be printed in every Soviet publication except certain works intended for export. It normally appears on the last printed page, or, if not, on the verso of the title-page. It contains, in a slightly varying order, certain bibliographical data (including the full names of the author(s) where personal authorship is attributed), and also data on the printing and publishing process for the work concerned. The example overleaf is typical.

The price of a book is also usually shown in the top left-hand corner of the outside back cover. Soviet publications in languages other than Russian usually contain a Russian colophon giving, among other information, a Russian translation of the title.

Many modern Soviet books also print a facsimile catalogue entry for the work (according to Soviet bibliographical conventions) on the verso of the title-page or accompanying the colophon. A large number also print, in one or other of these places, a paragraph outlining the contents and intended readership of the book.

Валентин Иванович Петров

ОТРАЖЕНИЕ СТРАНОЙ СОВЕТОВ
НАШЕСТВИЯ ГЕРМАНСКОГО ИМПЕРИАЛИЗМА В 1918 ГОДУ

Утверждено к печати Институтом истории СССР Академии наук СССР

Редактор издательства З. Г. Демидова. Художник М. К. Шевцов
Художественный редактор Н. А. Фильчагина. Технический редактор
З. Б. Павлюк. Корректоры Р. В. Молоканова, Н. А. Несмеева

ИБ № 18181

Сдано в набор 16.01.80. Подписано к печати 31.03.80. Т-05256.
Формат 84×108¹/₃₂. Бумага типографская № 1. Гарнитура обыкновенная.
Печать высокая. Усл. печ. л. 21,8. Уч.-изд. л. 24,9 Тираж 3400 экз.
Тип. зак. 2717. Цена 2 р. 80 к.

Издательство «Наука» 117864 ГСП-7, Москва, В-485, Профсоюзная ул., 90
2-я типография издательства «Наука» 121099, Москва, Г-99, Шубинский
пер., 10

$$\Pi \frac{10604-106}{042(02)-80} 54-80 \qquad \copyright \text{ Издательство «Наука», 1980 г.}$$

Translation:

Valentin Ivanovich Petrov [author's full name].

The repulse delivered by the land of the Soviets to the invasion by German imperialism in 1918 [title].

Confirmed for printing by the Institute for the History of the USSR of the Academy of Sciences of the USSR.

Publishing-house editor Z. G. Demidova. Designer M. K. Shevtsov. Design editor N. A. Fil'chagina. Technical editor Z. B. Pavlyuk. Proof-readers R. V. Molokanova, N. A. Nesmeeva.

Information form No. 18181 [submitted to State Committee for Publishing].

Sent for typesetting 16.1.80. Signed for printing 31.3.80. T-05256 [censorship serial number].

Format 84x108$\frac{1}{32}$. Printing paper No. 1. Normal typeface. Relief printing. Standard printer's sheets 21.8. Publisher's sheets 24.9. Edition size 3400 copies. Printers' order no. 2717. Price 2 roubles 80 kopeks. [Name and address of publishers and printers. Book-trade classification. Copyright statement.]

5.13. Serials

Most regular Soviet periodicals now carry an International Standard Serial Number (ISSN), but all those available for subscription also bear (usually on the back cover or last page) an index-number (индекс) which identifies the title for subscription purposes and should be quoted when ordering.

Many Soviet institutions publish regular or irregular serials of the 'proceedings' or 'transactions' type, characterized by such titles as бюллете́нь, ве́домости, ве́стник, докла́ды, запи́ски, изве́стия, сбо́рник, сообще́ния, or труды́. Identification and recording of these publications is often difficult: an institution may produce several such serials, each title sometimes being itself no more than a series title comprising several subject sections, which may split, re-form and divide again on a different pattern; numbering may be inconsistent or, particularly for early volumes, non-existent (see 5.11); and finally, the definition of some of them as serials at all may be open to doubt where the publishing institution's intentions are unclear. Headings for such serials with 'non-distinctive' titles would be subject to AACR2, 21.1B2.

Further reading

Turchyn, A. 'Slavic publications: their cataloging and classification in American libraries'. In: Aman, Mohamed M., ed. *Cataloging and classification of non-Western material.* Phoenix/Lond., Oryx Press/ Library Association, 1980, pp. 297-320.

Section 6

BIBLIOGRAPHIES AND REFERENCE WORKS

This chapter gives an introduction to:

6.1. Current bibliographies of Soviet publications.
6.2. Retrospective bibliographies and catalogues useful for the identification of works in Russian.
6.3. Quick-reference works in English giving useful information on Russia and the USSR.
6.4. Russian-English dictionaries, general and specialized.

6.1. Current bibliographies

Current bibliographical coverage is now provided for most kinds of Soviet publication. The Soviet current national bibliography of books (*Knizhnaya letopis'*), its annual cumulation (*Ezhegodnik knigi SSSR*), and the weekly lists of forthcoming books and of works just published (*Novye knigi SSSR* and *Knizhnoe obozrenie*, respectively) are described below in some detail, and Soviet national bibliographies for other categories of publication more briefly. In all these bibliographies, entries are in Russian throughout: entries for works printed in other languages are given in Russian translation, with a (very inconspicuous) note of the language of publication.

6.1.1. *Knizhnaya letopis'* ⸻⸻⸻⸻⸻⸻⸻⸻
(*Кни́жная ле́топись: Book chronicle*)

This bibliography of books and pamphlets published in the Soviet Union appears in two 'issues' (вы́пуски). The 'basic issue' (основно́й вы́пуск) appears weekly and contains primarily material intended for a relatively wide readership, including nearly all titles available through the commercial book trade. Nevertheless, it also records many noncommercial publications obviously intended for a limited circulation.

The 'supplementary issue' (дополни́тельный вы́пуск) appears monthly in two separate sections, entitled respectively *Кни́ги и брошю́ры* ('Books and pamphlets') and *Авторефера́ты диссерта́ций* ('Dissertation summaries'). The former is a selective listing of works expected to be of interest to a limited range of readers, including many official publications, conference proceedings, trade catalogues, instructional and technical material, and industrial manuals. The latter lists the pamphlet-size summaries which are printed for Soviet higher-degree dissertations.

Both 'issues' include material printed in all languages and published anywhere in the USSR. They exclude 'ephemera', works 'intended for a very limited readership', and publications of less than five pages or produced in under 100 copies. Entries usually appear in *KL* several months after publication of the work to which they refer, which limits its usefulness as a selection tool.

Arrangement of the basic issue and the first section of the supplementary issue is into 50 main subject classes with extensive further subdivision. Individual entries generally follow the order and format of the General International Standard Bibliographical Description (ISBD(G)), with some additional data at the end of each entry. For examples see the extract overleaf. Single volumes of a series or multi-volume set are when necessary given an individual description following that of the series or set as a whole.

Indexes to the basic issue and the first section of the supplementary issue are published in separate quarterly numbers, each containing name, geographical, and (in the basic issue only) subject indexes, but no title index. There is an annual index to series, published separately for each issue. References in all indexes are only to entry number, which often necessitates the chasing of several entry numbers back to weekly issues in search of further details.

30675. **Тойм К.** Теоретические основы психометрии : Учеб. пособие для студентов психол. отд-ния. — Тарту : ТГУ, 1981. — 78 с.; 20 см. — В надзаг.: Тарт. гос. ун-т. Эст. Библиогр.: с. 75—77. — 15 к. 500 экз. — [82-7476] п оп

15.001.§

30676. **Факторович А. А., Постников Г. И.** Защита городов от транспортного шума. — Киев : Будівельник, 1982. — 142 с., ил.; 21 см. — На корешке 2-й авт.: П. [!] И. Постников. Библиогр.: с. 139—141 (62 назв.) — 65 к. 7.000 экз. — [82-40048] п тп

625.098 (-21)

4 АТЕИЗМ. РЕЛИГИЯ

30679. **Становление и развитие массового атеизма в западных областях Украинской ССР** / [Ю. Ю. Сливка, С. Т. Боруцкий, В. А. Голяк и др.]. — Киев : Наук. думка, 1981. — 255 с.; 20 см. — Авт. указаны на обороте тит. л. В надзаг.: АН УССР, Ин-т обществ. наук. Укр. — В пер. : 2 р. 20 к. 1.200 экз. — [82-9249] п тп

215 (477.8) (091)

Translation of Knizhnaya letopis' extract:

30675. Toim K. Theoretical bases of psychometrics: text-book for students of the Psychological Department. – Tartu: TGU (ie Tartu State University), 1981. – 78 pp.; 20 cm. – At head of title: Tartu State University. In Estonian. Bibliography: pp. 75-77. – 15 kopeks. 500 copies. – [82-7476] (ie Book Chamber index number). 1st ed. Reproduced from typewriting. UDC classification.

30676. Faktorovich A. A., Postnikov, G. I. The protection of towns against transport noise. – Kiev: Budivel'nik, 1982. – 142 pp., illus.; 21 cm. – On spine 2nd author: P. [!] I. Postnikov. Bibliography: pp. 139-141 (62 titles). – 65 kopeks. 7000 copies. – [82-40048] 1st ed. Printed from typesetting. UDC classification.

4 ATHEISM. RELIGION

30679. The beginnings and development of mass atheism in the western districts of the Ukrainian SSR / [Yu. Yu. Slivka, S. T. Borutskii, V. A. Golyak and others]. – Kiev: Naukova dumka, 1981. – 255 pp.; 20 cm. – Authors shown on verso of title-page. At head of title: Academy of Sciences of the Ukrainian SSR, Institute of Social Sciences. In Ukrainian. – In hard cover : 2 roubles 20 kopeks. 1200 copies. – [82-9249] 1st ed. Printed from typesetting. UDC classification.

6.1.2. *Ezhegodnik knigi SSSR*

(*Ежегóдник кнúги СССР: Book annual of the USSR*)

This is an annual publication cumulating the entries in the basic issue *only* of *Knizhnaya letopis'*, but further excluding reissues of school textbooks and irregular series of the *trudy* type without individual titles (the latter are recorded in *LPPI SSSR:* see 6.1.5). For retrospective reference (not selection) it is far more convenient to use than the multitude of *KL* weekly issues.

Arrangement is into the same 50 subject classes as in *KL*, but since 1957 *EK* has appeared each year in two volumes, of which the first now contains classes 1-14 and 42-50 (ie the social sciences and humanities) and the second, classes 15-41 (the natural sciences and technology). Layout of entries is an abbreviated version of that in *KL*.

Indexes are given in each volume for: names; titles occurring as headings (another advantage over *KL*); works in non-Russian languages; translations; and subjects.

6.1.3. *Novye knigi SSSR*

(*Нóвые кнúги СССР: New books of the USSR*)

This is a weekly, selective catalogue of forthcoming books, intended as a tool for selection by non-Soviet buyers, and as such of value due to the difficulty of obtaining Soviet books even immediately after publication. It gives a far from comprehensive picture of works in preparation, emphasizing books expected to appeal to readers abroad and giving very limited coverage to those printed in languages other than Russian. There are no indexes. The length of advance notice varies from zero to well over a year, since many issues incorporate much of the contents of publishing-houses' full annual plans. The average contents is rather over 300 new titles per issue. Price and length of books are always provisional unless announced after publication.

Arrangement is chiefly by subject classes, but under a system rather different from that of *KL* and *EK*. There are sometimes special sections, and occasionally special issues, devoted to a single publishing-house or subject. The headings most regularly occurring are:

Содержáние (Contents)

Срóчная информáция (Quick information. Works just published or
    about to be published, and not previously announced, often in con-
    nection with special occasions such as Party congresses).

Гото́вятся к вы́пуску (Being prepared for publication).

Обще́ственно-полити́ческая и социа́льно-экономи́ческая литерату́ра (Socio-political and socio-economic literature. Includes history, politics, international relations, economics and planning).

Есте́ственные нау́ки. Матема́тика (Natural sciences. Mathematics).

Те́хника. Промы́шленность. Тра́нспорт (Technology. Industry. Transport).

Нау́чные непериоди́ческие продолжа́ющиеся изда́ния (Scholarly irregular serials. Volumes in numbered series only).

Се́льское хозя́йство (Agriculture).

Здравоохране́ние. Медици́на (Public health. Medicine).

Физи́ческая культу́ра. Спорт (Physical culture. Sport).

Нау́ка. Культу́ра. Просвеще́ние (Scholarship. Culture. Education).

Печа́ть. Книгове́дение. Библиоте́чное де́ло. Библиогра́фия (The press. Study of books. Librarianship. Bibliography).

Худо́жественная литерату́ра (Literature, ie belles-lettres).

Де́тская литерату́ра (Childrens' literature).

Иску́сство. Искусствове́дение (Art. Art studies. Includes theatre).

Изобрази́тельная проду́кция (Illustrative publications, eg reproductions, volumes consisting chiefly of illustrations).

Уче́бная литерату́ра (Educational literature. Textbooks and instructional materials. Includes sections on language-learning material).

Переопубликова́ние (Reissue. Titles announced previously and now intended for reprinting. Orders, and/or confirmation of orders sent for the original issue, are invited).

Вы́шли из печа́ти (Issued from the press. Items already published).

Предлага́ются впервы́е (Offered for the first time. New publications, often from provincial publishers, not previously announced in *NK*).

Предлага́ются повто́рно (Offered again. Titles announced previously, now in print and stated to be still available. Orders invited).

Информа́ция (Information. Often announcements of major new multi-volume works for subscription).

Измене́ния в назва́нии, объёме и сто́имости книг (Changes in the titles, sizes and prices of books).

It was formerly *NK*'s custom to publish, at the end of an issue, occasional lists of titles which had been announced but had not, in the event, reached publication. This useful practice appears now (1982) to have been at least temporarily abandoned.

Кирпотин В. Мир Достоевского. Исследования, статьи. (05). Изд. 2-е, доп. «Сов. писатель». 25 л. 20 000 экз. 2 р. 10 к. II квартал 1983 г. 46 01 48 2002083.
В книге известного советского литературоведа В. Я. Кирпотина исследуются существенные идейно-художественные особенности творчества Ф. М. Достоевского. Работы, включенные в книгу, посвящены главным образом рассмотрению изученных произведений и персонажей Ф. М. Достоевского. Переиздание книги. В переплете.
НК № 36—82 г. (16)

Translation of Novye knigi SSSR extract:
Kirpotin V. The world of Dostoevsky. Researches, articles. (05). 2nd ed., enlarged. "Soviet Writer" (publishing-house). 25 sheets (approx. 400 pp.). 20,000 copies. 2 roubles 10 kopeks. 2nd quarter of 1983. 46 01 48 2002083 (ie book-trade reference no.)

In this book by the well-known Soviet literary critic V. Ya. Kirpotin are studied important ideological and artistic features in the creative work of F. M. Dostoevsky. The publications included in the book are devoted chiefly to the examination of F. M. Dostoevsky's widely studied works and characters. Reissue of the book. In hard cover. NK No. 36-82 (16).

6.1.4. *Knizhnoe obozrenie* _____

(*Кни́жное обозре́ние: Book survey*)
This is a newspaper-format weekly, published jointly by the State Committee for Publishing and the All-Union Voluntary Society of Booklovers. Its main value for the book selector lies in its weekly list of 350-450 new book titles issued by Soviet publishing-houses, entitled 'Knigi nedeli' ('Books of the week'). Titles are listed on receipt of copies by the journal's office, often well before they appear in the bookshops, and usually several months before they are recorded in an issue of *Knizhnaya letopis'*. Ordering from *KO* is likely to have a better chance of success than ordering from *KL*, and in some cases better even than from *Novye knigi SSSR*, especially when requesting on exchange from Soviet libraries — many of which will have received copies for their 'exchange stock' at much the same time as they appear in *KO*.

The list is limited to works issued by publishing-houses proper (ie excluding material produced by government organs, research institutes, etc), and to those published in 1000 or more copies and at least one printer's sheet (usually 16 pages) in length. It should not be assumed to be exhaustive even within these limits, but is nevertheless extensive and useful, including for example a much higher proportion than *NK* of titles in languages other than Russian. Arrangement is by broad subject classes similar to those used in *Knizhnaya letopis'*, with particulars of each book given in a highly abbreviated form. Titles in series available on subscription are marked by a black spot, and those in non-Soviet languages and intended for libraries only are given in two separate sections at the end of each list. Items are not numbered, and no indexes are provided.

6.1.5. Other current Soviet national bibliographies

The following are the remaining components in the USSR's all-Union bibliographical coverage, recording most of the country's non-monographic printed output. All are published by the All-Union Book Chamber (Всесоюзная книжная палата) in Moscow.

Letopis' periodicheskikh i prodolzhayushchikhsya izdanii SSSR
(*Лётопись периодических и продолжающихся изданий СССР –*
ЛППИ: 'Chronicle of periodical and serial publications of the USSR') provides a full listing of Soviet regular and irregular serials (*not* their contents). A complex publishing history (it has borne its present title since 1971), but basically consists of a complete listing at five-yearly (for 1955-60, six-yearly) intervals, with annual supplements of varying coverage. The latter consisted in 1982 of three publications: for collections of articles (сборники), bulletins (бюллетени) and for journals and newspapers newly established, ceasing publication or changing their title.

Letopis' zhurnal'nykh statei *(Лётопись журнальных статей:*
'Chronicle of journal articles') is a weekly index to articles in selected serials, regular and irregular, published in the USSR *in Russian.* Over 2000 serials are now indexed per year, yielding some 4000 index entries in each issue. The emphasis is on scholarly material, and coverage of journals published in the peripheral republics, and of irregular series, is very selective. Subject arrangement, with name and geographical indexes published every two months and an annual index to source titles.

Letopis' retsenzii (*Лётопись рецёнзий:* 'Chronicle of reviews') is a monthly bibliography of selected reviews published in the serials indexed by *Letopis' zhurnal'nykh statei* and *Letopis' gazetnykh statei*, and in certain local papers. It has separately published annual indexes.

Letopis' gazetnykh statei (*Лётопись газётных статёй:* 'Chronicle of newspaper articles') is a selective weekly index to articles, documents and literary works published in Russian in 39 Soviet newspapers (in 1982). *Pravda* and *Izvestiya* are the most thoroughly covered. Subject arrangement, with name and geographical indexes in each issue.

Letopis' izoizdanii (*Лётопись изоиздáний:* 'Chronicle of illustrative publications') is a monthly record of printed illustrative material. It includes posters, reproductions, art-quality postcards, and 'albums' (альбóмы), ie books consisting principally or entirely of art reproductions or photographs. The latter are also included in *KL*.

Notnaya letopis' (*Нóтная лётопись:* 'Chronicle of music') is a monthly bibliography of music published in the USSR.

Kartograficheskaya letopis' (*Картографи́ческая лётопись:* 'Cartographic chronicle') is an annual bibliography, in two parts, of atlases and separately published maps.

6.2. Retrospective bibliographies and catalogues

Apart from the back runs of the works listed in the preceding section, retrospective identification of Russian and Soviet publications is catered for by a large number of bibliographies and catalogues which, nevertheless, even taken together, do not provide a total coverage. Most of the works concerned are listed (though without notes or commentary) in:

Simmons, J. S. G. *Russian bibliography, libraries and archives.* Oxford/[Twickenham, A. C. Hall], 1973. xviii, 76 pp.

A second edition is in preparation. A well-annotated, although now far from up-to-date, selective guide is:

Horecky, P. L. *Basic Russian publications. An annotated bibliography on Russia and the Soviet Union.* Chicago, UP, 1962. xxvi, 313 pp.

The most comprehensive catalogue devoted to Russian (and other Cyrillic) publications is:

Library of Congress. *The Slavic Cyrillic union catalog of pre-1956 imprints.* Totowa, NJ, Rowman & Littlefield, 1980. 174 microfiches and 36-pp. booklet.

The SCUC contains nearly 400,000 cards, including serials, for holdings at the Library of Congress itself and some 220 other North American libraries. Alphabetical author/title arrangement.

One of the most important single Slavonic collections is catalogued in:

New York Public Library. Reference department. *Dictionary catalog of the Slavonic collection.* 2nd ed. Boston, G. K. Hall, 1974. 44 vols.

Both the SCUC and the NYPL catalogues are brought up to date, as far as American holdings are concerned, by the later volumes of the *National union catalog.* The largest Russian collection in the United Kingdom is that of the British Library Reference Division (in large part that of the former British Museum Library), which is recorded in the BM's *General catalogue of printed books*, its supplements, and most recently in:

The British Library catalogue of printed books to 1975. London, Bingley/Saur, 1979-

A large number of Soviet official publications (in a very wide definition of that term) from 1945 are listed in Jenny Brine's chapter (pp. 263-559) in:

Walker, G., ed. *Official publications of the Soviet Union and Eastern Europe.* London, Mansell, 1982. xxviii, 620 pp.

A very extensive bibliography of Soviet serials (within its chronological limits) is:

Smits, R. *Half a century of Soviet serials 1917-1968. A bibliography and union list of serials published in the USSR.* Washington, Library of Congress, 1968. 2 vols.

This lists both regular and irregular serials, with a thorough statement of issues published in each case. It is complemented by:

Schatoff, M. *Half a century of Russian serials 1917-1968. Cumulative index of serials published outside the USSR.* Ed. by N. A. Hale. New York, Russian Book Chamber Abroad, 1970-72. 4 vols.

6.3. Quick-reference works in English

An up-to-date encyclopaedia devoted solely to Russia and the USSR is:

The Cambridge encyclopaedia of Russia and the Soviet Union. Gen.
eds. A. Brown [et al.]. Cambridge UP, 1982. 492 pp.

Still useful for many subjects, and for short biographies, is:

Utechin, S. V., ed. *Everyman's concise encyclopedia of Russia.*
London, Dent, 1961. xxvi, 623 pp.

Giving far more extensive treatment of most topics relating to the
USSR, albeit from an official Soviet standpoint, is the English translation of the latest edition of the *Bol'shaya sovetskaya entsiklopediya*:

Great Soviet encyclopedia. A translation of the third edition. New
York/London, Macmillan/Collier Macmillan, 1973-   .

This will be completed in 30 volumes, each a translation of one of the
Russian volumes, with all the problems of alphabetical arrangement
arising from this policy.

Two more specialized encyclopaedias, now in progress and each to
consist of about 50 volumes on completion, are:

Wieczynski, J. L., ed. *The modern encyclopedia of Russian and
Soviet history.* Gulf Breeze, Fla., Academic International Press,
1976-   .

Weber, H. B., ed. *The modern encyclopedia of Russian and Soviet
literature.* Gulf Breeze, Fla., Academic International Press, 1977-   .

A highly compressed but very wide-ranging annual, devoted principally to recent events and statistics, is:

USSR facts and figures annual. Ed. by J. L. Scherer. Gulf Breeze,
Fla., Academic International Press, 1977-   .

It also includes name lists, chronologies and short background surveys.
The latter especially vary in subject-matter from year to year, and not
all tables, etc, are annually updated.

The most accessible source of 'directory'-type data on Soviet cultural
and academic institutions is the section devoted to the USSR published
in:

World of learning. London, Europa, annual.

This gives brief data on academies, learned societies, archives, libraries,
museums, higher education and research institutions. Addresses, and
often leading staff members, are shown. Not exhaustive, nor always
entirely up to date.

Biographical information on Russian and Soviet figures, besides
appearing in all the encyclopaedias mentioned above, can also be found

(for individuals from the post-revolutionary period) in the two following works:

>*Who's who in the socialist countries.* Eds. B. Lewytzkyj &
>J. Stroynowski. NY/München, K. G. Saur/Vlg Dokumentation,
>1978. 736 pp.

>*Who was who in the USSR.* Ed. by H. E. Schulz et al. Metuchen,
>NJ, Scarecrow Press, 1972. 677 pp.

The former gives brief career summaries and publication lists for some 10,000 individuals in 15 other communist countries besides the USSR, with some emphasis on Party and government figures. The latter provides similar data for over 5,000 persons prominent in the Soviet Union between 1917 and 1967, including some 'anti-Soviet' figures.

6.4. Russian-English dictionaries

>*The Oxford Russian-English dictionary.* By M. Wheeler. Gen. ed.
>B. O. Unbegaun. Oxford, Clarendon Press, 1972. 918 pp.

Now the standard work for general use. About 70,000 entries. New edition in preparation.

>*Russian-English dictionary.* Under the general direction of A. I.
>Smirnitsky. 11th, stereo. ed. Moscow, Russkii Yazyk, 1977. 766 pp.

New 'editions' (usually impressions) appear at intervals. About 50,000 words.

>Borkowski, P. *The great Russian-English dictionary of idioms and
>set expressions.* London, the author, 1973. xvi, 384 pp.

Over 8600 Russian entries. Alphabetical arrangement by catchword system.

>*Slovar' sokrashchenii russkogo yazyka.* Izd. 2-e, ispr. i dop. [by]
>D. I. Alekseev, I. G. Gozman, G. V. Sakharov. Moskva, Russkii
>yazyk, 1977. 414 pp.

No English, but useful for its 15,000 abbreviations.

>Crowe, B. *Concise dictionary of Soviet terminology, institutions
>and abbreviations.* Oxford, Pergamon, 1969. 182 pp.

About 1700 'Sovietisms', emphasizing those most common in Soviet literature, with explanations designed for English readers.

>Smith, R. E. F. *A Russian-English dictionary of social science terms.*
>London, Butterworths, 1962. xii, 495 pp.

Covers sociology, politics, economics, public administration and education. Somewhat dated but still very useful. Over 9000 entries.

Pushkarev, S. G. *Dictionary of Russian historical terms from the 11th century to 1917.* Yale UP, 1970. xi, 199pp.

Terminology of politics, law, society, economics, finance, taxation, offices and ranks. Many definitions are long, with historical explanations and quotations. About 1500 terms.

Russian-English bookman's dictionary. Comp. by T. P. Elizarenkova, ed. by B. P. Kanevsky. Moscow, Soviet Encyclopedia, 1969. 264 pp.

Of particular value to librarians, containing 9300 terms from bibliography, librarianship, publishing, printing, the book trade and (to a limited extent) information science. Lack of recent terminology is an increasing handicap.

Russko-angliiskii politekhnicheskii slovar'. Pod. red. B. V. Kuznetsova. Moskva, Russkii yazyk, 1980. 723 pp.

About 90,000 terms from science and technology, with special emphasis on mathematics, statistics, information theory, computers, electronics and engineering.

Further reading

On Soviet national bibliographies:

Whitby, T. J. & Lorković, T. *Introduction to Soviet national bibliography.* Littleton, Colo., Libraries Unlimited, 1979. 229 pp.

A brief history and current account (at 1976-77) of Soviet national bibliographical development, followed by a translation of a Soviet work of *1967*, acting as a guide to the organs of national and republic-level bibliography at that time.

On dictionaries, W. F. Ryan's well-informed chapter 'Russian: Dictionaries' in:

Walford, A. J. & Screen, J. E. O., eds. *A guide to foreign language courses and dictionaries.* 3rd ed., rev. & enl. London, Library Association, 1977, pp. 186-195.

A regular review article, 'Reference materials in Russian-Soviet area studies', by Wojciech Zalewski, has appeared in the quarterly *Russian review* each year since 1975, dealing with publications from 1973 onwards.

Section 7

OTHER LANGUAGES USING THE
CYRILLIC ALPHABET

Six other European languages besides Russian use the Cyrillic alphabet. Of the three spoken within the USSR, Ukrainian and Belorussian are closely related to Russian linguistically, and these languages together make up the East Slavonic branch of the Slavonic (or Slavic) group of languages. Moldavian is virtually identical with Romanian, which uses the Roman alphabet. Outside the Soviet Union, Serbian, Macedonian and Bulgarian are all South Slavonic languages, and the latter two are particularly close to each other.

The list below gives recognition features by which to distinguish these six languages from Russian: differences in alphabets and common linguistic features, vernacular names for the nationalities and localities concerned, and the towns most frequently occurring as places of publication.

Ukrainian
The letters є and ï are peculiar to the language. i now occurs only in Ukrainian and Belorussian.

УРСР: Ukrainian SSR (*not* the Union of Soviet Socialist Republics). Україна, український: Ukraine, Ukrainian.

Київ (Kiev). Харків (Khar'kov). Львів (L'vov). Одеса (Odessa). Ужгород (Uzhgorod). Пряшів (Prešov, Czechoslovakia).

Emigré publishing in Ukrainian is active in several countries, notably Canada, the USA, the UK and the Federal Republic of Germany.

Belorussian (or Byelorussian)
The letter ў is peculiar to the language. и and щ are not used, being rendered by i and шч.

БССР: Belorussian SSR. Беларусь, беларускі: Belorussia, Belorussian.

Мінск (Minsk).

Moldavian

The endings -y, -ул, -лор, and -pe are characteristic, also the auxiliary words луй, ла, де, ши.

PCCM: Moldavian SSR. Молдова, молдовенеск: Moldavia, Moldavian.

Кишинэу (Kishinev).

Serbian

Although to all intents and purposes the same language, the Serbo-Croat spoken in the Yugoslav republics of Serbia, Bosnia-Hercegovina and Montenegro is written in Cyrillic and often described simply as Serbian, while that spoken in the republic of Croatia uses the Roman alphabet and often the names Croato-Serbian, Croat or Croatian.

In Cyrillic, Serbian is characterized by the letters ħ and ђ. j, љ, њ and џ are common to Serbian and Macedonian.

СФРЈ: Socialist Federal Republic of Yugoslavia. Југославија, југословенски: Yugoslavia, Yugoslav. Србија, српски: Serbia, Serbian. Босна, босански: Bosnia, Bosnian. Црна Гора, црногорски: Montenegro, Montenegrin.

Београд (Belgrade). Нови Сад (Novi Sad). Сарајево (Sarajevo). Титоград (Titograd). Цетиње (Cetinje).

There is a limited amount of émigré publishing, mostly in the USA.

Macedonian

ѓ, ѕ and ќ are peculiar to the language. j, љ, њ and џ occur in Macedonian and Serbian only. Definite articles are added as suffixes to the *end* of a noun or adjective as they are in Bulgarian. In Macedonian they are most often -от, -та, -то, -те.

Македонија, македонски: Macedonia, Macedonian.

Скопје (Skopje).

Bulgarian

The letter ъ, while not unique to Bulgarian, now occurs far more frequently in that language (where it has roughly the sound of '-er' in 'bitter') than in any other language currently using Cyrillic. Suffixed definite articles occur as in Macedonian, their most frequent Bulgarian forms being -ът, -та, -то, and -те.

НРБ: People's Republic of Bulgaria. България, български: Bulgaria, Bulgarian.

София (Sofia). Пловдив (Plovdiv). Варна (Varna).

Others

Less likely to be encountered by most librarians are Soviet publications in those non-European languages of the USSR which employ Cyrillic, although in all cases with additional or modified characters. The most widely spoken are Uzbek, Kazakh, Azerbaidzhani, Tadzhik, Turkmen, Tatar and Kirghiz. In most non-periodical publications, the colophon (see 5.12) will furnish a Russian translation of the title and a note in Russian of the language used in the text.

VOCABULARIES

8.1. Guide to word endings

The grammatical form in which words are entered in these vocabularies (as in dictionaries) is standardized as the nominative singular of nouns, the nominative singular masculine of adjectives and the infinitive of verbs. The most common variant endings are listed below, with a key to the form of ending which will be found in the vocabulary and dictionary entry.

Ending	If not in dictionary, try under:	Grammatical explanation
none	-а, -о	noun: gen. pl. fem. or neut.
-а (see also -ла)	none or -о	noun: gen./acc. sg. masc., gen. sg. neut. or nom. pl. neut.
-ам	none, -а, -о	noun: dat. pl.
-ами	none, -а, -о	noun: instr. pl.
-ах	none, -а, -о	noun: loc. pl.
-ая	-ый	adj.: nom. sing. fem.
-е (see also -ее, -ие, -ое, -ые)	none, -а, -я or -о	noun: loc. sing., or dat. sing. fem.
-его	-ий	adj.: gen./acc. sg. masc., gen. sg. neut.
-ее	-ый, -ий	adj.: comparative form or nom./acc. sg. neut.

Ending	If not in dictionary, try under:	Grammatical explanation
-ей	-я, -ь, -е	noun: instr. sg. fem., or gen. pl. fem. or neut.
-ем	{ -й, -е { -ий	noun: instr. sg. masc. or neut. adj.: loc. sing. masc. or neut.
-ему	-ий	adj.: dat. sg. masc./neut.
-и (see also -имн, -ки, -ли, -ыми)	none, -а, -я, -ь, -е	noun: gen. or loc. sg. fem., loc. sg. neut., nom./acc. pl. masc., nom. pl. fem.
-ие	-ий	adj.: nom./acc. pl.
-ий	-ия, -ие	noun: gen. pl. fem. or neut.
-им	-ий	adj.: instr. sg. masc./ neut., dat. pl.
-ими	-ий	adj.: instr. pl.
-их	-ий	adj.: gen. or loc. pl., or acc. pl. masc.
-ки	-кий	adverb: derived from adj. (see 1.5.4)
-л, -ла, -ло, -ли, -лся, -лась, -лось, -лись	-ть, -ться	verb: past tense (see 1.10.3, 1.10.4)
-о (see also -его, -ло, -ого)	-ый	adverb: derived from adj. (see 1.5.4)
-ов	none	noun: gen./acc. pl. masc.
-ого	-ый	adj.: gen./acc. sg. masc. or gen. sg. neut.

Ending	If not in dictionary, try under:	Grammatical explanation
-ое	-ый	adj.: nom./acc. sg. neut.
-ой	{ -ый -a	adj.: gen./dat./instr./ loc. sg. fem. noun: instr. sing. fem.
-ом	{ none or -o -ый	noun: instr. sg. masc. or neut. adj.: loc. sg. masc. or neut.
-ому	-ый	adj.: dat. sg. masc. or neut.
-ою	-ый	adj.: instr. sg. fem.
-у (see also -ему, ому)	none, -o, -a	noun: dat. sg. masc. or neut., acc. sg. fem.
-ую	-ый	adj.: acc. sing. fem.
-ы	none, -a, -o	noun: nom. pl. masc. or fem., gen. sg. fem.
-ые	-ый	adj.: nom./acc. pl.
-ым	-ый	adj.: instr. sg. masc. or neut., or dat. pl.
-ыми	-ый	adj.: instr. pl.
-ых	-ый	adj.: gen. pl. or acc. pl. masc.
-ью	-ь	noun: instr. sg. fem.
-ю (see also -ую, -ью)	-я, -e	noun: acc. sg. fem., dat. sg. neut.
-я	-й, -e	noun: gen./acc. sg. masc., gen. sg. neut. or nom. pl. neut.
-ям	-й, -я, -ь, -e	noun: dat. pl.
-ями	-й, -я, -ь, -e	noun: instr. pl.
-ях	-й, -я, -ь, -e	noun: loc. pl.

8.2. Alphabetical vocabulary

This lists all the Russian words used in the linguistic section of the book, and a selection of others likely to be of use to the librarian. It omits abbreviations and the names of publishing-houses, which are given in separate lists.

а	and, but
абонемент	loan, lending, circulation
август	August
автор	author
автореферат	synopsis of dissertation/thesis
адрес	address. по адресу: to the address
азербайджанский	Azerbaidzhani (adj.)
академик	academician (ie member of an Academy of Science, Medicine, etc. The title carries high prestige
академия	academy
Алма-Ата	Alma-Ata (capital of the Kazakh SSR)
алфавитный	alphabetical
альбом	album, volume of illustrations (applied especially to lavishly illustrated large-format works)
альманах	anthology, literary miscellany
английский	English
Англия	England
аннотация	annotation
аннотированный	annotated
аннулировать	to cancel, annul
апрель	April
Армения	Armenia
армянский	Armenian
архив	archives
Ашхабад	Ashkhabad (capital of the Turkmen SSR)
Баку	Baku (capital of the Azerbaidzhani SSR)
бандероль	wrapper; 'printed matter', 'book post' (on parcels or packets)
без	(with gen.) without
Белороссия	Belorussia, White Russia
белорусский	Belorussian, White Russian
бесплатно	free of charge, unpriced

библиографи́ческий	bibliographical	Великобрита́ния	Great Britain
библиогра́фия	bibliography	ве́стник	bulletin;
библиоте́ка	library		messenger
библиоте́чный	library (adj.)	весь, вся,	all
биографи́ческий	biographical	всё, все	
биогра́фия	biography	верхо́вный	supreme.
блокно́т	notebook;		Верхо́вный
	writing pad		Сове́т
бо́лее	more		Supreme
большеви́к	Bolshevik		Soviet.
большо́й	great, big		Верхо́вный
брошю́ра	booklet,		Суд Supreme
	pamphlet		Court
букле́т	(illustrated)	Ви́льнюс	Vilnius (capital
	booklet,		of the Lithu-
	pamphlet		anian SSR)
бума́га	paper (ie for	вклад	contribution
	printing or	включа́ть	to contain
	writing, *not*	(ipfve),	
	a newspaper)	включи́ть	
буржуа́зный	bourgeois	(pfve)	
быть	to be	включи́тельно	inclusive (adv.)
бюллете́нь	bulletin	власть	power
		вме́сто	(with gen.)
			instead of
в	(with acc.) into,	внима́ние	attention
	at; (with loc.)	во	[variant of в]
	in, at	вопро́с	question,
ва́жный	important		matter
ваш	your, yours	восемна́дцать	eighteen
введе́ние	introduction	во́семь	eight
ве́домость	list, register;	во́семьдесят	eighty
	(pl.) record,	воспомина́ние	memory;
	gazette		(pl.) memoirs
ве́домственный	departmental,	восто́к	east, the Orient
	official	восто́чный	eastern,
век (nom. pl.	century, age,		Oriental
века́)	era	восьмо́й	eighth
вели́кий	great	впервы́е	for the first time

вре́мя (nom. pl. вре́мена)	time	гравю́ра	engraving, print
все, вся	all	грамма́тика	grammar
всесою́зный	all-Union (ie applying to the entire USSR)	гра́фика	graphic production
вспомога́тельный	auxiliary, additional	грузи́нский	Georgian
вступи́тельный	introductory, opening	Гру́зия	Georgia
второ́й	second (ie 2nd)	да́льний	distant, far
вуз	higher educational institution	два, две	two
		два́дцать	twenty
		двена́дцать	twelve
вы	you	две́сти	two hundred
вы́йти (pfve)	to go out, appear, be published	девяно́сто	ninety
		девятна́дцать	nineteen
		девя́тый	ninth
вы́пуск	issue, number; instalment, fascicule	де́вять	nine
		дека́брь	December
		де́ло	affair, matter, business
высо́кий	high	день (nom. pl. дни)	day
вы́сший	higher		
выходи́ть (ipfve)	to go out, appear, be published	деся́тый	tenth
		де́сять	ten
		де́тский	childrens'
		диссерта́ция	dissertation, thesis
газе́та	newspaper	для	(with gen.) for
где	where	дневни́к	diary
глава́	chapter; head, chief (noun)	до	(with gen.) until, up to
гла́вный	main, principal, head (adj.)	добавле́ние	addition, appendix, addendum
год	year		
го́род	town, city	докла́д	report, address, paper, lecture
госуда́рственный	state (adj.)		
		до́ктор	doctor (as a higher-education degree, usu.
госуда́рство	state (noun)		
гото́вить (ipfve)	to prepare; (-ся) to be prepared		

	equated with the British or American 'higher doctorates')	еженедельный	weekly (adj.)
должно́ быть	should be	её	her, hers; it, its
дом (nom. pl. дома́)	house	Ерева́н	Erevan (capital of the Armenian SSR)
доокти́брьский	pre-October (ie of 1917)	ещё	still, yet
дополне́ние	supplement		
допо́лненный	supplemented	же	[emphatic particle, used in
дополни́тельный	supplementary		constructions such as он же
дореволюцио́нный	pre-Revolutionary (ie before the 1917 October Revolution)		ibid., там же loc. cit., того́ же а́втора by the same author]
доце́нт	senior lecturer (in higher education)	жизнеописа́ние	biography
драматурги́я	the drama, playwriting	журна́л	periodical, journal
		журнали́стика	journalism
дре́вний	ancient		
друго́й	other(s)	за	(with acc.) for; during; behind. (with instr.) for; owing to; behind
Душанбе́	Dushanbe (capital of the Tadzhik SSR)		
евре́йский	Jewish; (of language) Yiddish	заве́дующий	head, manager, person in charge
Евро́па	Europe	загла́вие	title, heading
его́ (pron. ево́)	him, his; it, its	зада́ча	problem, task, object
ежего́дник	annual (noun)		
ежего́дный	annual (adj.)	Закавка́зье	Transcaucasia
ежеме́сячник	monthly (noun)	зака́з	order
ежеме́сячный	monthly (adj.)	заключе́ние	conclusion
еженеде́льник	weekly (noun)	зако́н	law

замести́тель	deputy (with gen., eg замести́тель дире́ктора)	и́мени	named after, named for (Amer.)
заме́тка	note, notice	именно́й	name (adj.)
за́пад	west, the West		именно́й указа́тель name index
за́падный	western		
запи́ска	note; (pl.) notes; transactions	и́ндекс	index (number)
за́пись	record, entry; recording, booking	иностра́нец	foreigner
		иностра́нный	foreign
		институ́т	institute
		информа́ция	information
зарубе́жный	foreign	испо́льзование	use, utilization, с испо́льзованием материа́лов using the materials (accumulated by X)
заседа́ние	session, sitting		
зая́вка	order, claim		
значе́ние	meaning, significance		
и	and, also		
идти́ (ipfve)	to go	исправле́ние	correction
из	(with gen.) from, out of	иссле́дование	investigation, research
и́збранный	selected	исто́рик	historian
изве́стия	news; transactions	истори́ческий	historic(al)
		исто́рия	history
извлече́ние	extract, excerpt	исто́чник	source
издава́ть (ipfve), изда́ть (pfve)	to publish. (-ся) to be published	ито́г	sum, total, result
		их	of them, their, theirs
изда́ние	edition, impression, publication (see 5.9)	ию́ль	July
		ию́нь	June
изда́тельство	publishing-house	к	(with dat.) to, up to, towards
измене́ние	alteration, change		
изобрази́тельный	figurative, illustrative	Кавка́з	Caucasus
		каза́хский	Kazakh (adj.)
изуче́ние	study (of a subject, etc)	как	how
и́ли	or	календа́рь	calendar
иллюстра́ция	illustration		

кандида́т	candidate (as a higher-education degree, usu. equated with the British or American Ph.D)	коллекти́в	collective, group
		комите́т	committee
		комму-нисти́ческий	Communist (adj.)
		компле́кт	(complete) set, full number
ка́рта	map; card	коне́ц (gen. sing. конца́)	end, finish
карти́на	picture, painting		
карто-графи́ческий	cartographic, map (adj.)	конча́ть (ipfve) ко́нчить (pfve)	to finish, end. (-ся) to be finished
ка́рточка	card (eg catalogue card)		
		копе́йка	kopek (1/100 of a rouble)
ка́федра	chair (in university); department, sub-faculty	корреспонде́нт	correspondent. член-корреспон-де́нт corres-ponding member (eg of Academy)
кварта́л	quarter (esp. of a year)		
Ки́ев	Kiev (capital of the Ukrainian SSR)		
		кра́ска	paint; (pl.) colour(s)
кирги́зский	Kirghiz (adj.)	кра́ткий	short
Кита́й	China	кро́ме	(with gen.) besides, except
кита́йский	Chinese		
Кишинёв	Kishinev (capital of the Molda-vian SSR)	Крым	the Crimea
		ксероко́пия	xerox copy, photocopy
кни́га	book	кто	who
книгове́дение	study of the book, biblio-logy	культу́ра	culture
		курс	course
книгоизда́-тельство	book publishing-house		
книгообме́н	book exchange	латви́йский	Latvian, Lettish
книготорго́вля	book trade	латы́шский	Latvian, Lettish
кни́жный	book (adj.), bookish		
ко	[variant of к]	лета́ (gen. pl. лет)	years
колле́гия	board, committee		

ле́топись	chronicle, annals	мно́го	much, many
лист	leaf; sheet of paper; printer's or publisher's sheet (usually equivalent to 16 printed pages)	мой, моя́, моё, мой	my, mine
		молда́вский	Moldavian
		моногра́фия	monograph (ie a work — often collective — devoted to a specific topic)
Литва́	Lithuania	Москва́	Moscow
литерату́ра	literature (not necessarily fiction)	моско́вский	Moscow (adj.), Muscovite
		музе́й	museum
лито́вский	Lithuanian	му́зыка	music
лу́чший	better, best	музыка́льный	musical
лю́ди	people	мы	we
		Мю́нхен	Munich
май	May	на	(with acc.) on to; (with loc.) on; and many other meanings in set phrases
ма́ленький	small, little		
март	March		
материа́л	material		
межбиблио-те́чный	inter-library. м. абонеме́нт inter-library loan		
		над	(with instr.) over, above
ме́жду	(with instr.) between, among	надзаголо́вок	head-of-title statement
		назва́ние	name, title
междуна-ро́дный	international	наименова́ние	name, designation, appellation
ме́нее	less		
ме́ньший	smaller	напеча́танный	printed
ме́сто	place, situation	написа́ть (pfve)	to write
		наро́д	people, nation
ме́сяц	month		
министе́рство	ministry	наро́дный	people's, popular, national
Минск	Minsk (capital of the Belorussian SSR)		

настоя́щий	present, current
нау́ка	science, scholarship (not restricted to natural science and technology)
нау́чно-иссле́до-вательский	scientific-research (adj.)
нау́чный	scientific, scholarly, academic
национа́льный	national, of nationalities (esp. of non-Russian minorities in the USSR)
нача́ло	beginning
наш	our, ours
не	not
неде́ля	week
неи́зданный	unpublished
не́который	some, certain
неме́цкий	German
непериоди́-ческий	irregular (of a journal or series)
не́сколько	several, a few
но	but
но́вый	new
но́мер	number; issue
но́та	musical note. (pl.) printed music
но́тный	musical
ноя́брь	November
о, об	(with acc.) against, along; (with loc.) about
обзо́р	survey, review
о́бласть	province, region, sphere
обло́жка	paper cover
обме́н	exchange
обозре́ние	review, survey
оборо́т	back, verso
обрабо́тать (pfve)	to work up/over, to process
обрабо́тка	working up/over, processing
обще́ственный	public, social
о́бщество	society, company
о́бщий	general, common, total
объём	size, amount
объя́вленный	announced
оглавле́ние	table of contents
оди́н, одна́, одно́	one
одина́дцать	eleven
о́коло	(with gen.) about, around
октя́брь	October
он, она́, оно́, они́	he, she, it, they
опеча́тка	misprint, erratum
описа́ние	description

опубликова́ть (pfve)	to publish. (-ся) to be published
о́пыт	trial, experiment, attempt
о́рган	organ (ie publication of an institution, etc)
организа́ция	organization
о́рден	order, decoration
осно́ва	basis, fundamental (noun)
основно́й	basic, fundamental (adj.)
осо́бенно	especially
от	(with gen.) from, away from
отве́тственный	responsible, in charge
отде́л (е́ние)	section, department
отде́льный	separate, detached
откры́тка	postcard
отноше́ние	attitude, relation(ship); (pl.) relations
отпра́вка	despatch, forwarding
отправля́ть (ipfve), отпра́вить (pfve)	to send, forward, despatch
о́трасль	branch, field, special sphere
о́ттиск	offprint; impression

отчёт	account, report
о́черк	outline, sketch, essay
паке́т	parcel, package
па́мятник	monument, relic
Пари́ж	Paris
па́пка	folder, document case
парти́йный	Party (adj.)
партиту́ра	musical score
па́ртия	(political) party. (In the USSR, usu. the Communist Party of the Soviet Union)
пе́рвый	first
перево́д	translation
переизда́ние	reprinting, republication
переимено́ванный	re-named
перепеча́тка	reprint
перепи́ска	correspondence
переплёт	binding, hard cover
перерабо́танный	revised, reworked
перерабо́тка	revision, reworking
пересмо́тренный	revised
пе́речень	list
периоди́ческий	periodical (adj.)
Петрогра́д	Petrograd (1914-1924)
печа́тный	printed

печа́ть	press; printing, print; seal, stamp	подтвержда́ть (ipfve), подтверди́ть (pfve)	to confirm
писа́тель	writer		
писа́ть (ipfve)	to write	политбюро́	the Politburo (of the Central Committee of the CPSU)
письмо́	letter		
плака́т	poster, wall sheet		
план	plan		
пле́нум	plenum, full meeting	по́лный	full
по	(with acc.) up to; (with dat.) because of, according to, along; (with loc.) after; and many other meanings in set phrases	положе́ние	position; standing, situation
		полуто́м	half-volume
		получа́ть (ipfve), получи́ть (pfve)	to receive
		получе́ние	receipt, receiving
		попра́вка	correction
по́весть	tale, story	поря́док	order; manner, procedure. в поря́дке обме́на on an exchange basis
повто́рно	again		
под	(with acc.) under (motion); (with instr.) under, below (position)		
		посвяще́ние	dedication
		посла́ть (pfve)	to send
подгото́вить (pfve)	to prepare; (-ся) to be prepared	по́сле	(with gen.) after
		после́дний	last, latest
подгото́вленный	prepared	послесло́вие	postscript, afterword
подобра́ть (pfve)	to select, pick	посо́бие	manual; aid, tool
подпи́ска	subscription	посыла́ть (ipfve)	to send
подписно́й	subscription (adj.), available on subscription	по́чта	post, mail
		поэ́зия	poetry

пра́вда	truth
предисло́вие	preface, foreword
предлага́ть (ipfve), предложи́ть (pfve)	to offer, propose
предме́т	article; object; subject, topic. предме́тный указа́тель subject index
предназна́-ченный	intended (for)
председа́тель	chairman
прекращённый	ceased, discontinued
при	(with loc.) at; in the time of; in the presence of; attached to
приложе́ние	appendix, supplement; enclosure (with a letter)
примеча́ние	note, comment
присыла́ть (ipfve), присла́ть (pfve)	to send
про	(with acc.) about, concerning; for
пробле́ма	problem
продолжа́ть (ipfve), продолжи́ть (pfve)	to continue. (-ся) to be continued
про́за	prose
произведе́ние	work, production
проспе́кт	prospectus
про́тив	(with gen.) against, opposite
профе́ссор	professor
про́чий	other
прочита́ть (pfve)	to read
публикова́ть (ipfve)	to publish. (-ся) to be published
публици́стика	essay-writing, journalism
путеводи́тель	guide (-book)
пье́са	play (theatrical)
пятиле́тка	five-year plan
пятна́дцать	fifteen
пя́тый	fifth
пять	five
пятьдеся́т	fifty
пятьсо́т	five hundred
рабо́та	work, activity
рабо́чий	working (adj.), worker (ie 'working person')
раз (gen. sg. ра́за, gen. pl. раз)	time, occasion
разви́тие	development
разгово́рник	phrase-book
разде́л	section, division; class
разрабо́тать (pfve)	to work out, elaborate
райо́н	region, district, area

распро́данный	disposed of, sold out	Росси́я	Russia
расска́з	story, tale	ротапри́нт	duplicator, mimeograph
рассчи́танный	intended (for)	рубе́ж	border. за рубежо́м abroad
расши́ренный	expanded, enlarged		
револю́ция	revolution	рубль	rouble
реда́ктор	editor	руково́дство	supervision, guidance, direction
редакцио́нный	editorial (adj.)		
реда́кция	editorial office/ staff; editorship	ру́копись	manuscript
		ру́сский	Russian (esp. of the Russian language and people)
ре́дкий	rare		
редколле́гия	editorial board		
резюме́	summary (often in another language)	Русь	Rus', (ancient) Russia
		с, со	(with acc.) about, approximately; (with gen.) from, off; (with instr.) with
рекомен- да́тельный	recommenda- tory		
репроду́кция	reproduction		
респу́блика	republic		
рефера́т	abstract; paper, essay	самизда́т	'self-publishing' (the unauthor- ized circulation of privately reproduced material)
реце́нзия	review		
речь	speech		
реше́ние	decision, resolution		
Ри́га	Riga (capital of the Latvian SSR)	са́мый	most; the very . . . ; same
рису́нок (nom. pl. рису́нки)	drawing	Санктпетер- бу́ргъ	St. Petersburg
роль	role, part	сбо́рник	collection, symposium, volume of articles
рома́н	novel		
росси́йский	Russian (esp. applied to the pre-1917 Russian Empire)		

сведе́ние	information; (pl.) particulars	соа́втор	co-author
сво́дный	combined, summary. сво́дный катало́г union catalogue	собра́ние	collection
		сове́т	soviet, council
		сове́тский	Soviet (adj.)
		совеща́ние	conference, meeting
свой, своя́, своё, свой	my (your, etc.) own, one's own	совреме́нный	contemporary
		содержа́ние	contents
связь	connection, link; communications	созы́в	convocation (eg of Supreme Soviet)
се́вер	north	сокращённый	abbreviated
се́верный	northern	сообще́ние	report, information, communication
седьмо́й	seventh		
сельскохозя́йственный	agricultural	со́рок	forty
		состави́тель	compiler, writer
семна́дцать	seventeen		
семь	seven	состави́ть (pfve), составля́ть (ipfve)	to compile
се́мьдесят	seventy		
сентя́брь	September		
середи́на	middle	соста́вленный	compiled
сери́йный	serial (adj.)	сотру́дник	collaborator; colleague, staff member
се́рия	series		
се́ссия	session, sitting		
Сиби́рь	Siberia		
систе́ма	system	социалисти́ческий	socialist (adj.)
сказа́ние	story, legend		
ска́зка	tale, story	социа́льный	social
славя́нский	Slavonic, Slavic	сочине́ние	work, composition
сле́довать (ipfve)	to follow	сою́з	union
		спи́сок	list
сле́дующий	following	спра́вочник	handbook, guide
слова́рь	dictionary		
сло́во	word	среди́	(with gen.) among, amidst
слу́жба	service		
со	[variant of с]		

сре́дний	middle (adj.)	твой, твоя́, твоё, твой	your(s)
ссы́лка	reference; exile, banishment	тво́рчество	creation, work
станда́рт	standard	теку́щий	current. теку́щий указа́тель литерату́ры current index to publications
стати́стика	statistics		
статья́	article		
стереоти́пный	stereotype(d)		
стиль	style		
стих	verse; (pl.) poetry		
стихотворе́ние	poem	темпла́н (from темат́ический план)	(long-term) plan, plan of subjects (esp. of publishing-houses)
сто	hundred		
сто́имость	cost, price, value		
столбе́ц (nom. pl. столбцы́)	column (typog.)		
		тетра́дь	writing-book, copy-book; fascicule, part
столе́тие	century		
страни́ца	page	те́хника	technology; technique
студе́нт	student		
счёт	reckoning, account	типогра́фия	printing-house
		тира́ж	size of edition, number of copies
съезд	congress		
		ти́тульный лист	title-page
табли́ца	table; plate (in book)	то́же	also, as well
		то́лько	only
таджи́кский	Tadzhik (adj.)	том (nom. pl. тома́)	volume
так	so, thus		
та́кже	also, as well		
Та́ллин	Tallinn (capital of the Estonian SSR)	торго́вля	trade, commerce. кни́жная торго́вля book-trade
Ташке́нт	Tashkent (capital of the Uzbek SSR)		
		тот, та, то, те	that
		тре́тий	third (3rd)
Тбили́си	Tbilisi (capital of the Georgian SSR)	треть	one-third ($\frac{1}{3}$)
		три	three
		три́дцать	thirty
		трина́дцать	thirteen

триста	three hundred	факту́ра	invoice, bill
труд	labour; (pl.) transactions	факульте́т	faculty, department (in higher education)
туркме́нский	Turkmen(ian) (adj.)		
ты	you (sing., familiar)	февра́ль	February
		филиа́л	branch (eg of institution or library)
ты́сяча	thousand		
у	(with gen.) by, at, near, in the possession of	фонд	stock; holdings, collection (in archive or library)
уже́	already	фотоко́пия	photocopy
узбе́кский	Uzbek (adj.)	Фра́нция	France
ука́занный	shown	францу́зский	French
указа́тель	index	Фру́нзе	Frunze (capital of the Kirghiz SSR)
указа́ть (pfve)	to show		
Украи́на	the Ukraine		
украи́нский	Ukrainian	фунт	pound. фунт сте́рлингов pound sterling
у́лица	street		
университе́т	university		
управле́ние	administration, directorate	футля́р	case, slipcase
уро́к	lesson		
уста́в	statutes, regulations, charter	хоро́ший	good
		хрестома́тия	collection of readings
утвержде́нный	confirmed, approved	худо́жест-венный	artistic, to do with the arts худо́жест-венная литерату́ра belles-lettres, fiction (not exclusively prose)
уче́бник	textbook, manual		
уче́бный	educational, training (adj.)		
учёный	learned, scholarly, academic (adj.); scholar (noun)		
уче́т	registration; stock-taking; accounting	худо́жник	artist, designer

цветно́й	coloured, colour (adj.)	шестна́дцать	sixteen
це́лый	whole, full	шесто́й	sixth
цена́	price	шесть	six
центра́льный	central	шестьдеся́т	sixty
ци́фра	figure, numeral, number	шко́ла	school
		экземпля́р	copy, specimen
часть	part, section	энциклопе́дия	encyclopaedia
челове́к	person, man	эпо́ха	epoch, age
чем	than	э́ра	era
че́рез	(with acc.) over, across, through	эсто́нский	Estonian
		э́тот, э́та, э́то, э́ти	this, these
чертёж	drawing, draft	юбиле́йный	anniversary, jubilee (adj.)
че́тверть	quarter (¼)	юг	south
четвёртый	fourth	ю́жный	southern
четы́ре	four		
честы́реста	four hundred	я	I
четы́рнадцать	fourteen	явля́ться (ipfve)	to be, serve as (followed by instr.)
чита́тель	reader		
чита́ть (ipfve)	to read		
член	member	язы́к	language
что (pronounced што)	what	янва́рь	January

8.3. Russian abbreviations

This list shows Russian abbreviations commonly encountered in bibliographical and library usage. Dictionaries listed in 6.4 will supply many
more.

авт.	author
азерб.	Azerbaidzhani (adj.)
АзССР	Azerbaidzhani Soviet Socialist Republic
акад.	academy
АН	Academy of Sciences
англ.	English
АПН	'Novosti' Press Agency
арм.	Armenian
АрмССР	Armenian Soviet Socialist Republic
АССР	Autonomous Soviet Socialist Republic
БАН СССР	Library of the Academy of Sciences of the USSR
б.г.	undated, n.d.
белор.	Belorussian
беспл.	free of charge, unpriced
б.и.	no publisher stated
библиогр.	bibliography, bibliographical
б-ка	library
б.м.	no place of publication stated, n.pl.
бр.	booklet, pamphlet
БСЭ	Great Soviet Encyclopedia
БССР	Belorussian Soviet Socialist Republic
б.ц.	unpriced
в.	century
вв.	centuries
ВИНИТИ	All-Union Institute for Scientific and Technical Information
включ.	inclusive
ВКП	All-Union Book Chamber
ВКП (б)	All-Union Communist Party (Bolsheviks) (1925-52)
вступ.	introductory, opening
ВТО	All-Union Theatre Society
вып.	issue, instalment, fascicule

г. (= год)	year
(= го́род)	town, city
ГАУ	Chief Directorate of Archives
ГБЛ	Lenin State Library of the USSR, Moscow
гг.	years
гл.	chapter; main, chief (adj.)
гос., госуд.	state (adj.)
ГПБ	Saltykov-Shchedrin State Public Library, Leningrad
ГПИ	State Pedagogical Institute
ГПНТБ СО АН СССР	State Public Scientific and Technical Library of the Siberian Department of the USSR Academy of Sciences
груз.	Georgian
Г (руз) ССР	Georgian Soviet Socialist Republic
ГУГК	Chief Directorate of Geodesy and Cartography
дис.	dissertation, thesis
д-р	Doctor
до н.э.	B.C.
доп.	supplement, supplementary, supplemented
доц.	senior lecturer (in higher education)
др.	other(s)
зав.	head, manager, person in charge
загл.	title, heading
зам.	deputy
и др.	and others, et al.
извлеч.	extract, excerpt
изд.	edition; impression; publication
изд-во	publishing-house
илл.	illustration(s)
им.	named after, named for
ИНИОН	Institute for Scientific Information in the Social Sciences (of the USSR Academy of Sciences)
ин-т	institute
иссл.	investigation, research
ист.	historic(al)
и т.д.	and so on, etc

к.	kopek (1/100 of a rouble)
каз.	Kazakh (adj.)
КазССР	Kazakh Soviet Socialist Republic
канд.	Candidate (higher-education degree)
каф.	chair, department, sub-faculty (in higher education)
кирг.	Kirghiz (adj.)
КиргССР	Kirghiz Soviet Socialist Republic
кн.	book
кн-во	book publishing-house
КНР	Chinese People's Republic
КПСС	Communist Party of the Soviet Union
л.	leaf; sheet of paper; printer's or publisher's sheet (usu. 16 pages)
Л.	Leningrad
лат(в).	Latvian, Lettish
ЛатвССР	Latvian Soviet Socialist Republic
ЛГУ	Leningrad State University
литов.	Lithuanian (adj.)
лит-ра	literature (not necessarily fiction)
ЛитССР	Lithuanian Soviet Socialist Republic
М.	Moscow
МБА	inter-library loan
м-во	ministry
МГУ	Moscow State University
мин-во	ministry
молд.	Moldavian (adj.)
МССР	Moldavian Soviet Socialist Republic
надзаг.	head-of-title statement
назв.	name, title
напеч.	printed
напр.	for example, eg
нар.	people's, popular, national
нем.	German (adj.)
НИИ	Scientific Research Institute
НТИ	scientific and technical information
н.э.	A.D.

обл.	
(= о́бласть)	province, region
(= обло́жка)	paper cover
о-во	society; company
оп	(abbreviation in *Knizhnaya letopis'*) printed by non-typographic means, usu. reproduced from typewriting
отв.	responsible, in charge
отд.	
(= отделе́ние)	section, department
(= отде́льный)	separate, detached
п	(abbreviation in *Knizhnaya letopis'*) first edition/impression
П., Пг.	Petrograd
пер.	
(= перево́д)	translation
(= переплёт)	binding, hard cover
поз.	item number
прим(еч).	note, comment
проч.	other(s)
р.	rouble
ред.	editor; editorial (adj.); editorial office/staff, editorship
РЖ	*Referativnyi zhurnal* ('Abstracts Journal')
рис.	drawing(s)
РСФСР	Russian Soviet Federated Socialist Republic (largest of the 15 union republics of the USSR)
рук.	supervision, guidance, direction
рус.	Russian
с.	page
сб.	collection, symposium, volume of articles
см.	
(= сантиме́тр)	centimetre
(= смотри́)	see, refer to
собр.	collection
сов.	Soviet (adj.)

сокр.	abbreviated, abbreviation
сост.	compiled, compiler
соц.	
(= социалисти́- ческий)	socialist (adj.)
(= социа́ль- ный	social
соч.	work, composition
Спб.	St. Petersburg
ср.	compare, cf.
СССР	Union of Soviet Socialist Republics, USSR
стлб.	column (typog.)
стол.	century
стр.	page
США	USA
т.	volume
тадж.	Tadzhik (adj.)
ТаджССР	Tadzhik Soviet Socialist Republic
т.е.	that is, ie
тип.	printing-house
тит. л.	title-page
тп	(abbreviation in *Knizhnaya letopis'*) printed from typesetting
ТССР	Turkmen(ian) Soviet Socialist Republic
туркм.	Turkmen(ian) (adj.)
тыс.	thousand
УДК	Universal Decimal Classification, UDC
узб.	Uzbek (adj.)
УзССР	Uzbek Soviet Socialist Republic
указ.	index
укр.	Ukrainian
ул.	street, road
ун-т	university
УССР	Ukrainian Soviet Socialist Republic (*not* Union of Soviet Socialist Republics)
фак.	faculty, department (in higher education)
фр.	French

ц.	price
ЦК	Central Committee
ЦСУ	Central Statistical Directorate
ч.	part, section
черт.	drawing, draft
экз.	copy, specimen
ЭССР	Estonian Soviet Socialist Republic
эст.	Estonian (adj.)
яз.	language

8.4. Soviet publishing-houses

This select list includes only the principal publishers of works in Russian (although some also publish in other languages), out of a total of over 200 publishing-houses at present (1982) functioning in the USSR. The house's subject range is noted where not evident from its title. All are located in Moscow except where otherwise stated.

Авро́ра	'Aurora'. Illustrated books in arts subjects, chiefly for export. (Leningrad).
АПН	Novosti Press Agency. Material on the contemporary USSR for foreign readers.
Воениздат	Publishing-House of the Ministry of Defence.
ВТО	All-Union Theatre Society. Plays, books on the theatre.
Вы́сшая шко́ла	'Higher School'. Textbooks, etc, for higher and secondary special education.
Гидрометеоиздат	Meteorology, hydrology, oceanography. (Leningrad).
ГУГК	Chief Directorate of Geodesy and Cartography. Maps and atlases.
Де́тская литерату́ра	'Childrens' Literature'.
Дони́ш	Publishing-House of the Tadzhik SSR Academy of Sciences (Dushanbe).
ДОСААФ	Popular works on military, scientific and technical subjects, also fiction.
Зина́тне	Publishing-House of the Latvian SSR Academy of Sciences. (Riga).
Зна́ние	'Knowledge'. Popular non-fiction, mainly in series.
Изда́тельство АН АрмССР	Publishing-House of the Armenian SSR Academy of Sciences. (Erevan).
Изда́тельство Каза́нского госуд. ун-та	Publishing-House of Kazan' State University. (Kazan').
Изда́тельство Ленингра́дского госуд. ун-та	Publishing-House of Leningrad State University. (Leningrad).
Изда́тельство Моско́вского госуд. ун-та	Publishing-House of Moscow State University.

114

Изда́тельство станда́ртов	Publishing-House for Standards.
Изобрази́тельное иску́сство	'Figurative Arts'.
Или́м	Publishing-House of the Kirghiz SSR Academy of Sciences. (Frunze).
Иску́сство	'Art'. Incl. works on theatre and cinema.
Кни́га	'Book'. Books, libraries, printing, bibliography.
Ко́лос	'Ear of Corn'. Agriculture.
Лёгкая и пищева́я промы́шленность	'Light and Food Industry'. Incl. textile and clothing industries.
Ленизда́т	Fiction and popular non-fiction, often with Leningrad theme. (Leningrad).
Лесна́я промы́шленность	'Timber Industry'.
Малы́ш	'Youngster'. Books for pre-school children (ie under 7 in the USSR).
Машинострое́ние	'Mechanical Engineering'.
Медици́на	'Medicine'.
Междунаро́дные отноше́ния	'International Relations'.
Металлу́ргия	'Metallurgy'. Incl. metal industries.
Мецниере́ба	Publishing-House of the Georgian SSR Academy of Sciences. (Tbilisi).
Мир	'World' (or 'Peace'). Scientific and technical books translated from foreign languages.
Мир и социали́зм	'Peace and Socialism'. International relations.
Мо́кслас	Publishing-House of the Lithuanian SSR Academy of Sciences. (Vilnius).
Молода́я гва́рдия	'Young Guard'. Publishing organ of the Communist Youth League (Komsomol).
Моско́вский рабо́чий	'Moscow Worker'. Large-circulation fiction and non-fiction.
Му́зыка	'Music'. Books and musical scores.
Мысль	'Thought'. Philosophy and social sciences.
Нау́ка (1)	'Science'. Publisher of the USSR Academy of Sciences. Scholarly works on all subjects. Separate offices for physical-mathematical literature (ФМЛ) and oriental literature (ВЛ). (Moscow, Leningrad, Novosibirsk).

Наýка (2)	Publishing-House of the Kazakh SSR Academy of Sciences. (Alma-Ata).
Наýкова дýмка	Publishing-House of the Ukrainian SSR Academy of Sciences. (Kiev).
Нéдра	'The Earth'. Geology, mining, oil and gas.
Педагóгика	'Pedagogics'. Educational theory and practice.
Политиздáт	Communist Party publisher. Political literature.
Прогрéсс	'Progress'. Socio-political literature in foreign languages and translated into Russian.
Просвещéние	'Education'. Text-books and supporting material for schools.
Профиздáт	Literature for and about trade unions.
Рáдио и связь	'Radio and Communications'. Including electronics, post and stamp collecting.
Рáдуга	'Rainbow'. Translations of Soviet literary and art works into foreign languages.
Россельхозиздáт	Agriculture.
Рýсский язы́к	'Russian Language'. Courses, grammars, dictionaries and A-V material for learning Russian.
Совéтская Россия	'Soviet Russia'. Russian fiction and classics, non-fiction with Russian themes.
Совéтская энциклопéдия	'Soviet Encyclopedia'.
Совéтский композитор	'Soviet Composer'. Musical books and scores.
Совéтский писáтель	'Soviet Writer'. Modern Soviet literature.
Совéтский худóжник	'Soviet Artist'. Soviet art.
Совремéнник	'Contemporary'. Modern RSFSR writers.
Стройиздáт	Construction industry, architecture, planning.
Судостроéние	'Shipbuilding'. (Leningrad).
Трáнспорт	'Transport'.
Фан	Publishing-House of the Uzbek SSR Academy of Sciences. (Tashkent).
Финáнсы и статистика	'Finance and Statistics'.
Физкультýра и спорт	'Physical Culture and Sport'.
Химия	'Chemistry'.

Худо́жественная литерату́ра	'Imaginative Literature'. Also criticism and literary history.
Худо́жник РСФСР	'Artist of the RSFSR'. (Leningrad).
Штии́нца	Publishing-House of the Moldavian SSR Academy of Sciences. (Kishinev).
Ылы́м	Publishing-House of the Turkmen SSR Academy of Sciences. (Ashkhabad).
Эконо́мика	'Economics'.
Элм	Publishing-House of the Azerbaidzhan SSR Academy of Sciences. (Baku).
Энергоизда́т	Power and energy industries, incl. nuclear.
Юриди́ческая литерату́ра	'Legal Literature'.

INDEX